Piano • Vocal • Guitar

TOP CHRISTIAN HITS

2017-2018

ISBN 978-1-5400-2326-1

HAL•LEONARD®
7777 W. BLUEMOUND RD. P.O. BOX 13819 MILWAUKEE, WI 53213

Visit Hal Leonard Online at
www.halleonard.com

ALL MY HOPE

Words and Music by DAVID CROWDER
and ED CASH

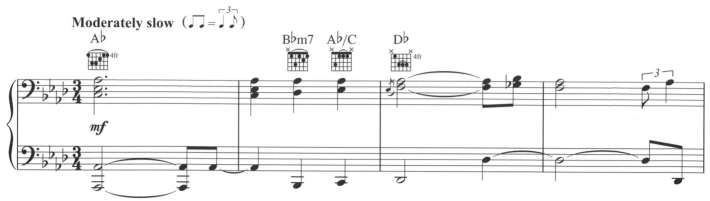

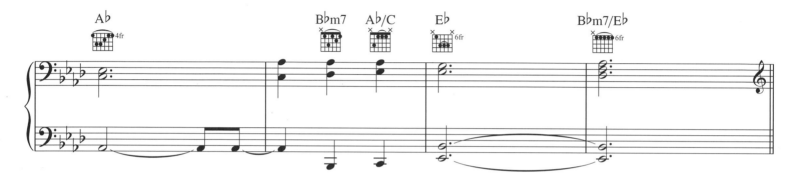

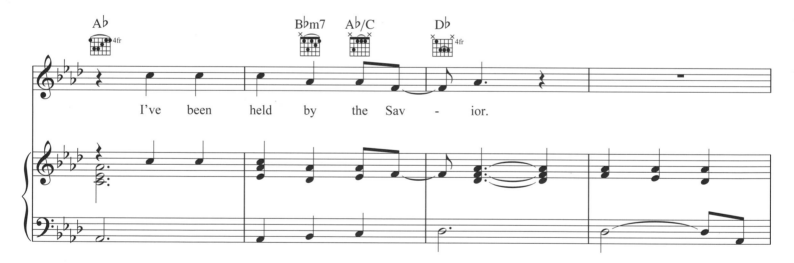

I've been held by the Sav - ior.

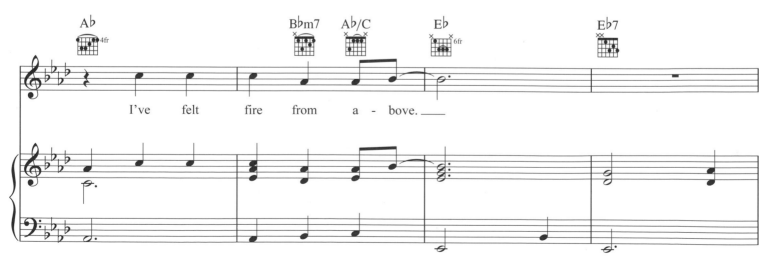

I've felt fire from a - bove.

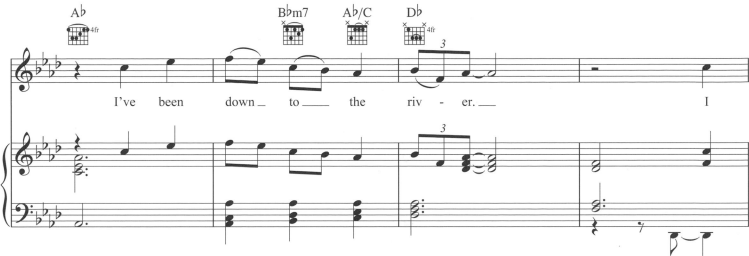

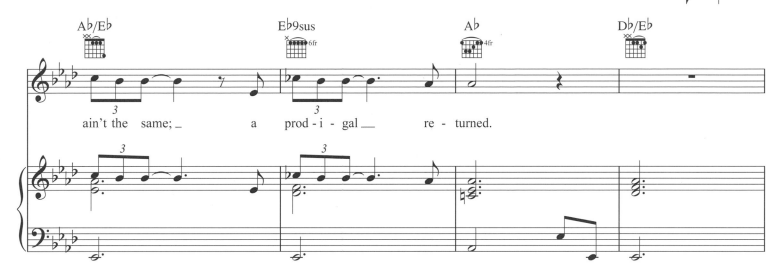

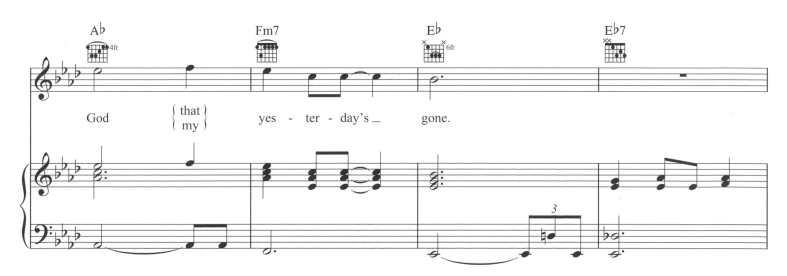

All my sins are for - giv - en, and

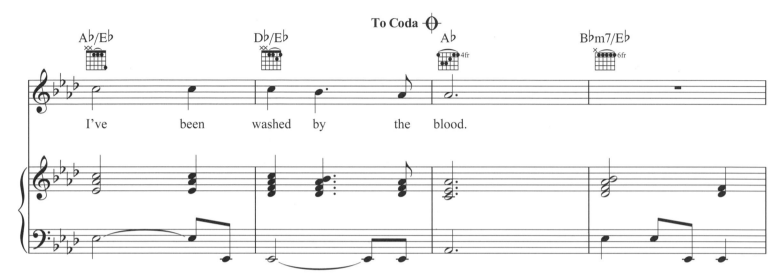

To Coda ⊕

I've been washed by the blood.

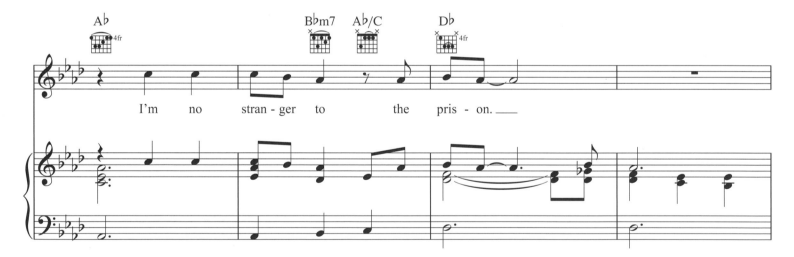

I'm no stran - ger to the pris - on.

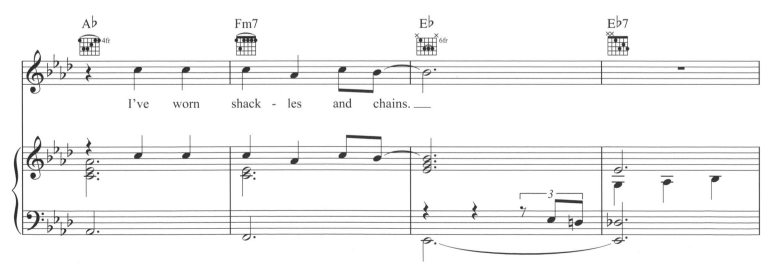

I've worn shack - les and chains.

But I've been freed_ and for - giv - en, ___ yes I have. I'm not

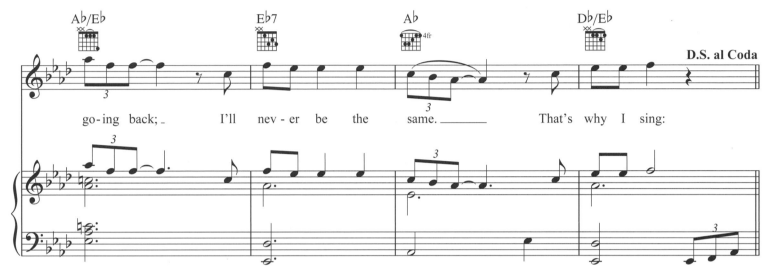

go - ing back; _ I'll nev - er be the same. ___ That's why I sing:

D.S. al Coda

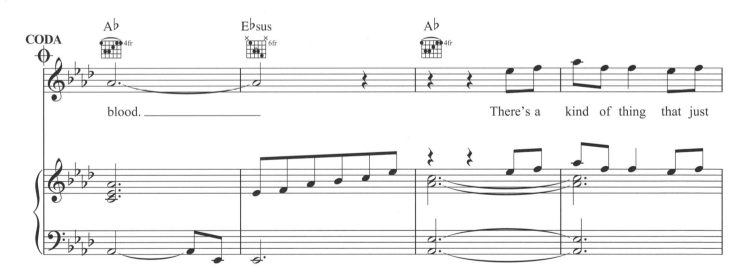

CODA

blood. ___ There's a kind of thing that just

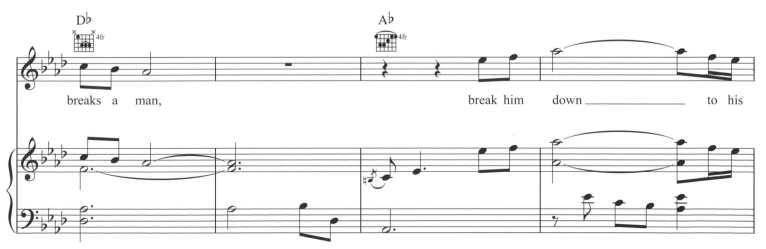

breaks a man, break him down ___ to his

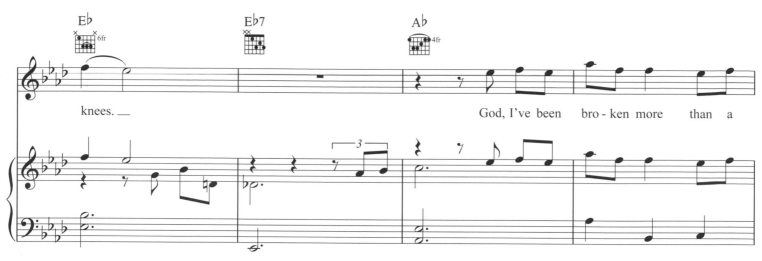

knees. __ God, I've been bro-ken more than a

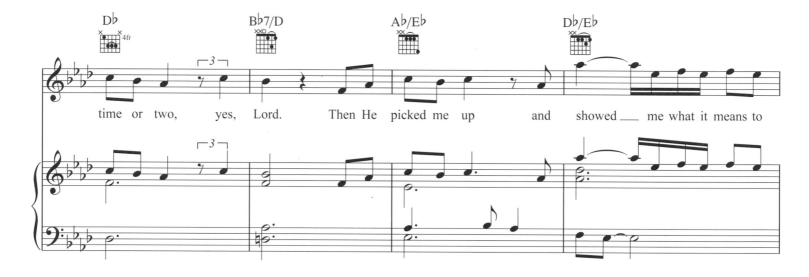

time or two, yes, Lord. Then He picked me up and showed __ me what it means to

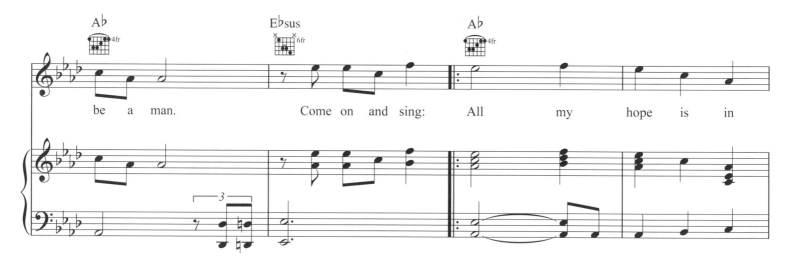

be a man. Come on and sing: All my hope is in

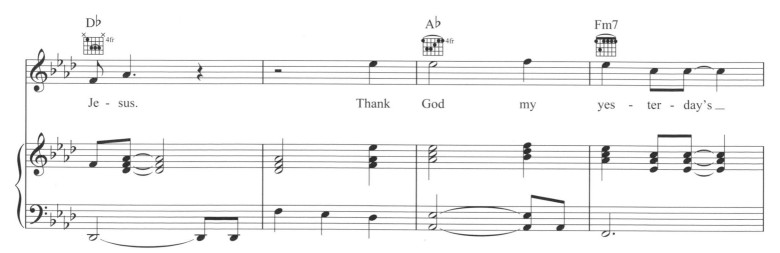

Je - sus. Thank God my yes - ter - day's __

BROKEN THINGS

Words and Music by MATTHEW WEST,
A.J. PRUIS and JASON HOUSER

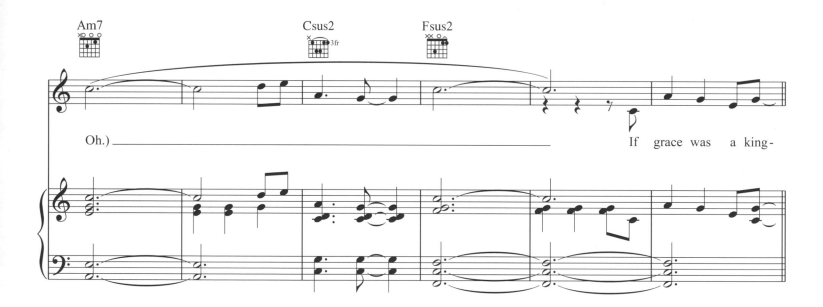

down. Said, "Child, don't you know _

Am7   C/G   Fsus2   G5

____ that the first ___ will be last, ___ and the last ___ get a crown?" _

C5   N.C.

___   And now,

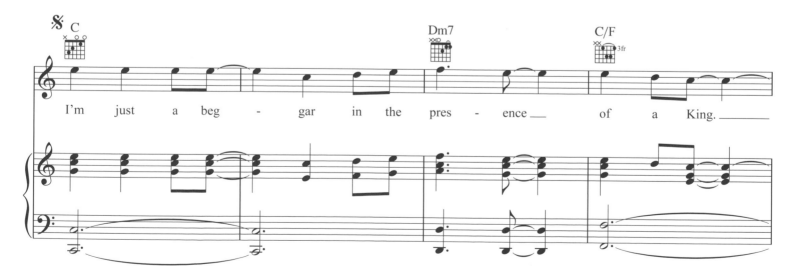

C   Dm7   C/F

I'm just a beg - gar in the pres - ence ___ of a King. _____

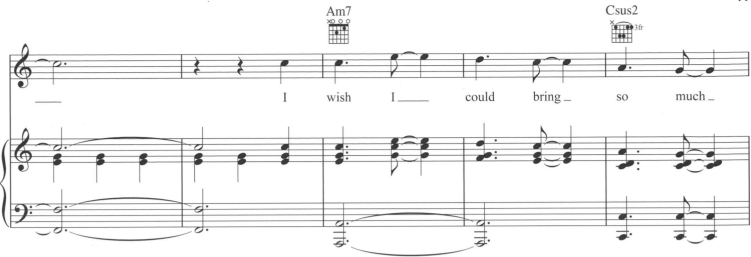

I wish I ___ could bring ___ so much ___

more. But if it's ___ true

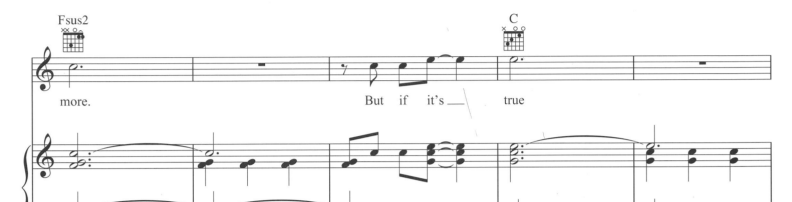

You use ___ bro - ken things, _____ then here I ___

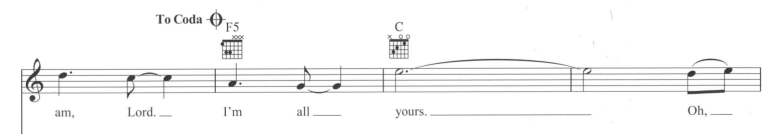

To Coda ⊕ F5

am, Lord. ___ I'm all ___ yours. _____ Oh, ___

whoa. _____

Oh. _____ The

pag - es of his - t'ry, _____ they

tell me it's ___ true, that it's

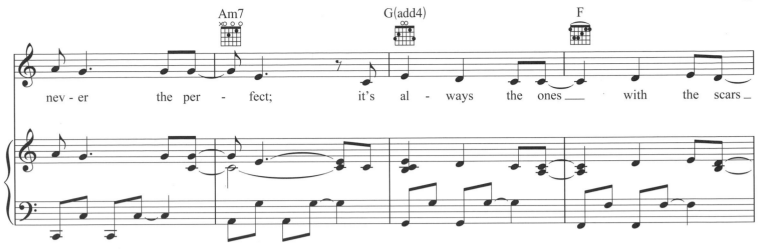

never the perfect; it's always the ones___ with the scars___

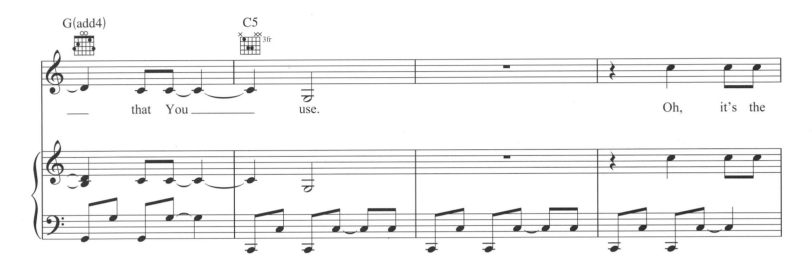

___ that You ___ use. Oh, it's the

reb - els and ___ the prod - i - gals,

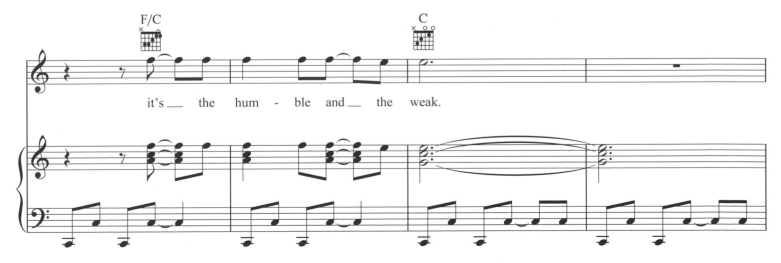

it's ___ the hum - ble and ___ the weak.

All __ the mis - fit __ he - roes You chose tell __ me

there's hope for sin - ners like _____ me. _____ And now,

I'm all __ yours. _____ Oh, __ whoa. _____

Oh.

EVEN IF

Words and Music by BART MILLARD,
DAVID GARCIA, BEN GLOVER,
TIM TIMMONS and CRYSTAL LEWIS

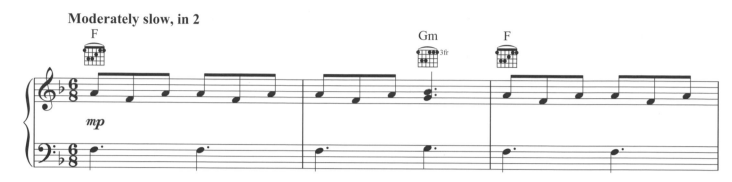

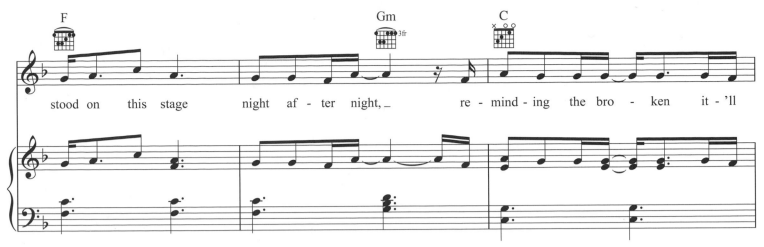

stood on this stage night af-ter night, _ re - mind-ing the bro - ken it - 'll

be al - right. _ But right now, _____ oh, right now, _ I just _____

___ can't. It's eas - y to sing _ when there's

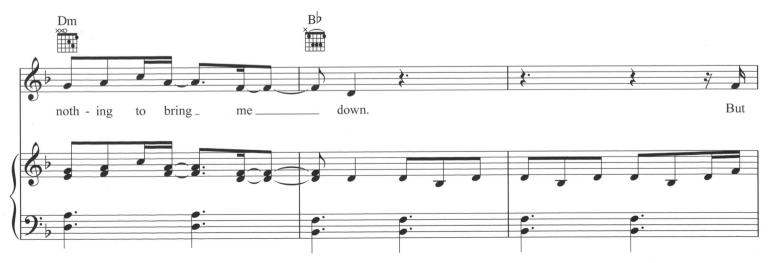

noth - ing to bring _ me _____ down. But

what will I sing____ when I'm held to the flame____ like I am right

now? I know You're a - ble and I_____ know You can____

save through the fi — re with Your____ might - y hand,___ but e - ven if You

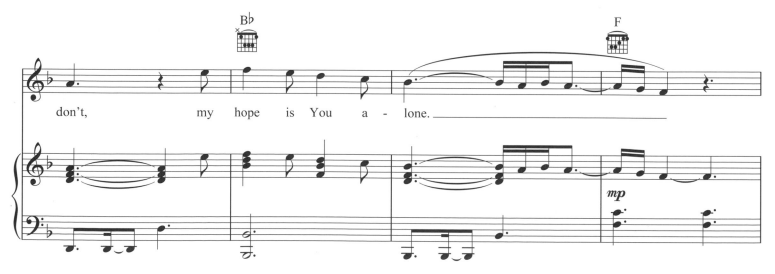

don't, my hope is You a - lone._____

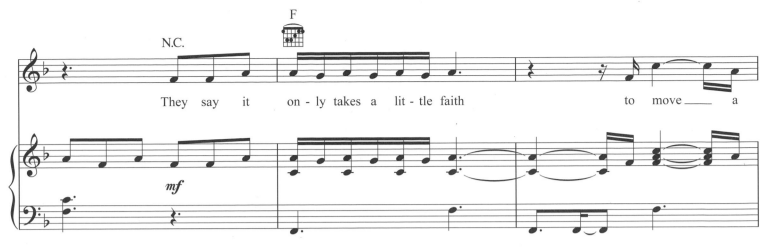

oh, ___ give me the strength ___ to be a-ble to sing, ___ "It is

well _____ with my soul." I know You're a - ble and I ___
I know the sor - row and I ___

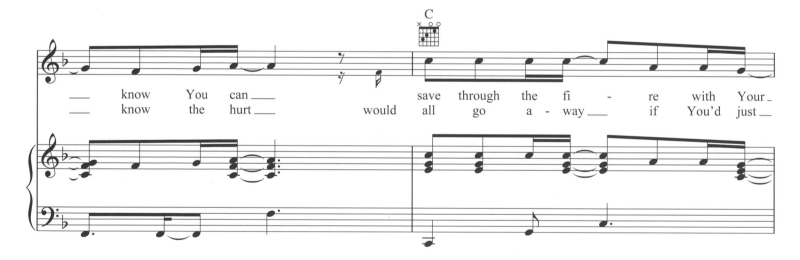

___ know You can ___ save through the fi - re with Your ___
___ know the hurt ___ would all go a - way ___ if You'd just ___

___ might - y hand, _} but e - ven if You don't, my
___ say the word, _}

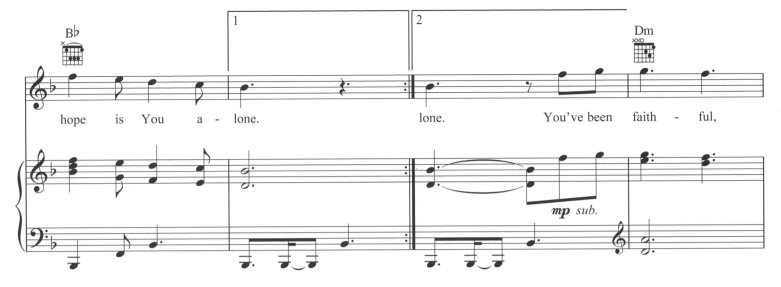

hope is You a - lone. lone. You've been faith - ful,

You've been good all of my days. Je - sus, I will

cling to You, come what may. 'Cause I know You're a - ble,

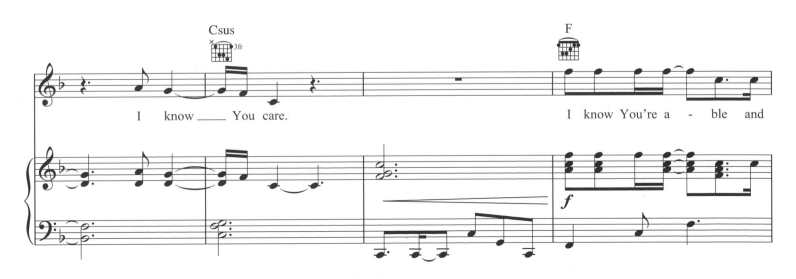

I know You care. I know You're a - ble and

I know You can ___ save through the fi - re with Your might - y hand, ___ but

e - ven if You don't, my hope is You a - lone. ___

I know the sor - row, I know the hurt ___ would all go a - way ___ if You'd

just say the word, ___ but e - ven if You don't, my hope is You a -

lone.

I hope in You a - lone, ooh, ooh.

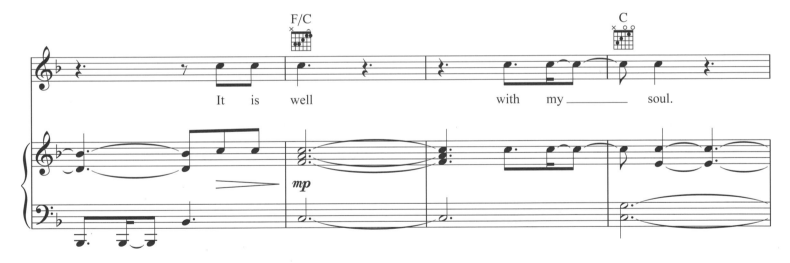

It is well with my _____ soul.

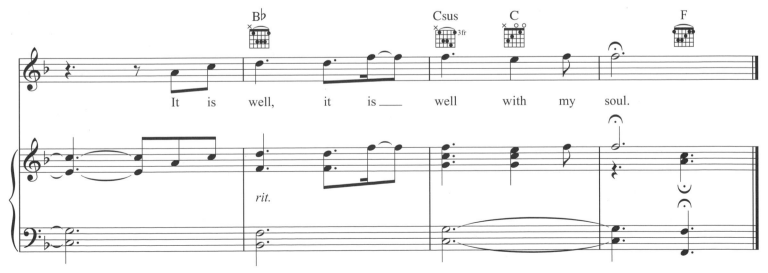

It is well, it is ___ well with my soul.

GOD OF ALL MY DAYS

Words and Music by JOHN MARK HALL
and JASON INGRAM

* Recorded a half step lower.

who makes all ___ things ___ new. I looked to You, ___
whose grace still cov - ers ___ me. I fell on You ___

drown - ing in ___ my ques - tions, and found the God ___
when I was at ___ my weak - est and found the God, ___

who holds all ___ wis - dom. And I trust - ed
the lift - er of my ___ head. And I've wor - shiped

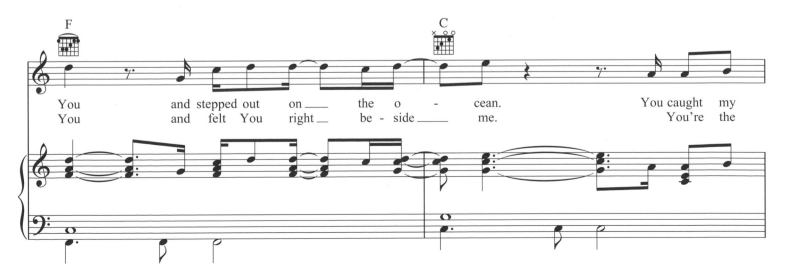

You ___ and stepped out on ___ the o - cean. You caught my
You ___ and felt You right ___ be - side ___ me. You're the

hand a-mong__ the waves,__ 'cause You're the God of__ all my__ days.__

rea-son that__ I sing,__ 'cause You're the God of__ all my__ days.__ Each step I__

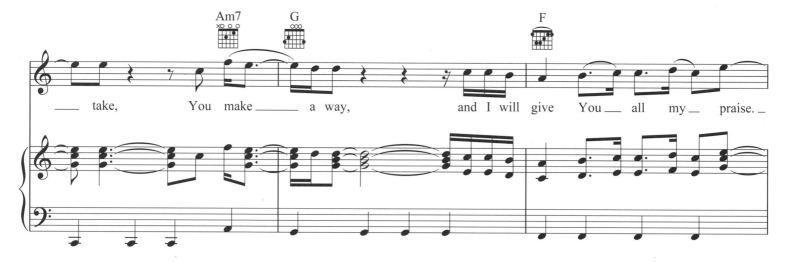

__ take, You make____ a way, and I will give You__ all my__ praise.__

__ My sea-sons__ change, You stay__ the same. You're the

To Coda ⊕

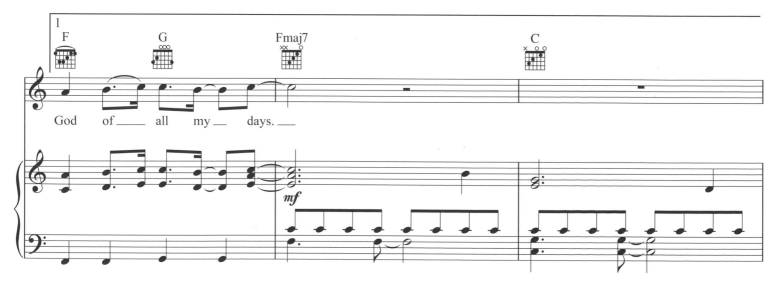

God of__ all my__ days.__

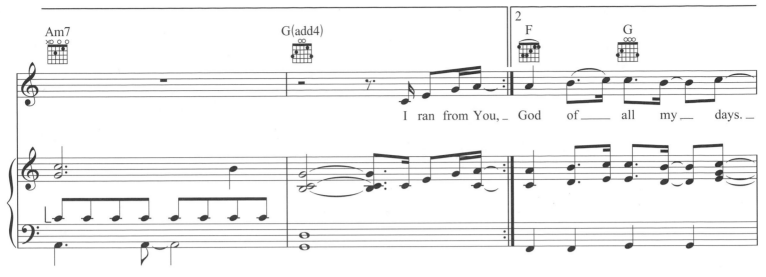

weak - ness, God, You are my pow - er. You're the rea-son that __ I sing, __ 'cause You're the

God of _____ all my __ days. __

D.S. al Coda

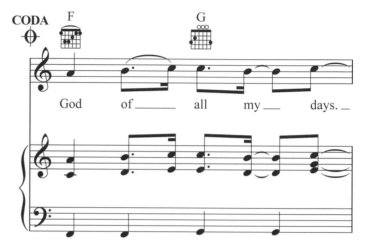

CODA

God of _____ all my __ days. __

In my blind - ness, God, You are my vi - sion. And in my

bond - age, God, You are my free - dom all my days.

BLEED THE SAME

Words and Music by CHRIS STEVENS,
BRYAN FOWLER, TOBY McKEEHAN
and MANDISA HUNDLEY

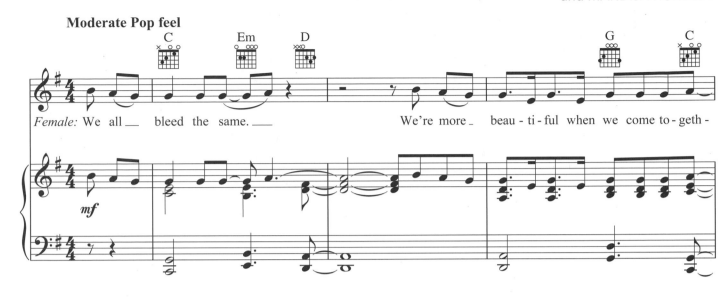

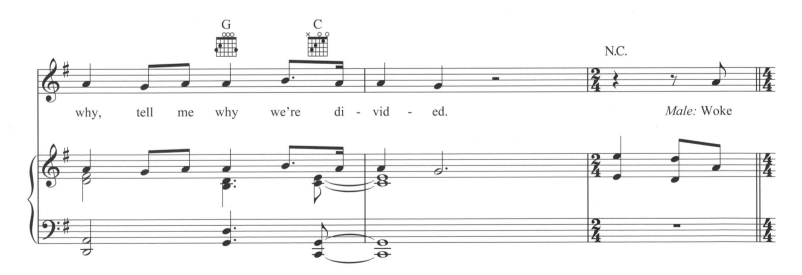

up to- day; _ an - oth - er head - line, _ an - oth - er in - no - cent life is

tak - en in the name of ha - tred. _ So hard to take, _ and if we

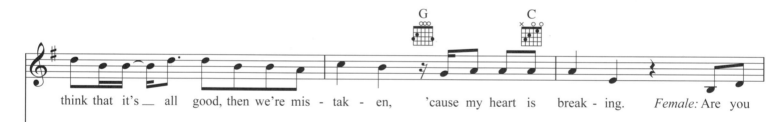

think that it's _ all good, then we're mis - tak - en, 'cause my heart is break - ing. *Female:* Are you

left? Are you right? Point - ing fin - gers, tak - ing sides. _ When are we gon - na re -

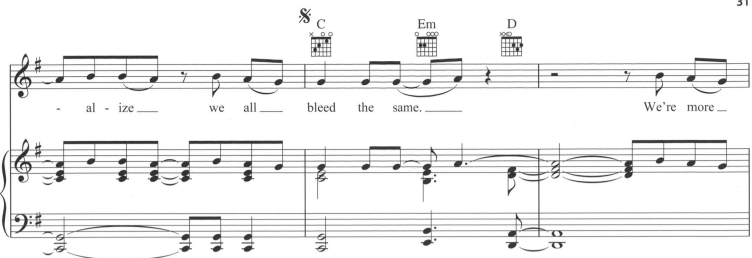

-al - ize ___ we all ___ bleed the same. ___ We're more ___

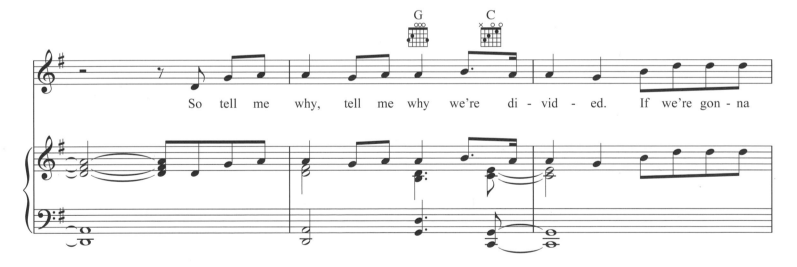

beau - ti - ful when we come to - geth - er. We all ___ bleed the same. ___

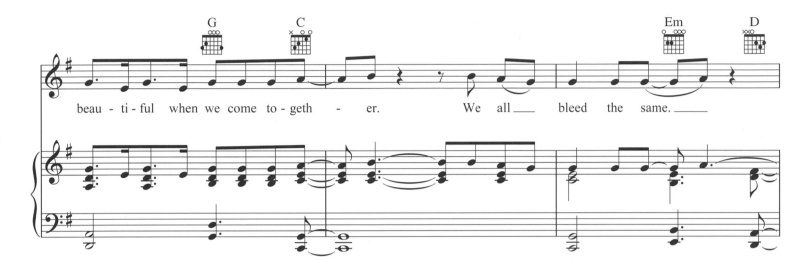

So tell me why, tell me why we're di - vid - ed. If we're gon - na

fight, let's fight for each oth - er. If we're gon - na shout, let love be the cry. ___

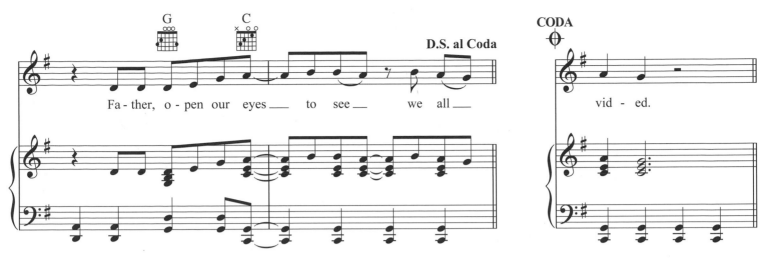

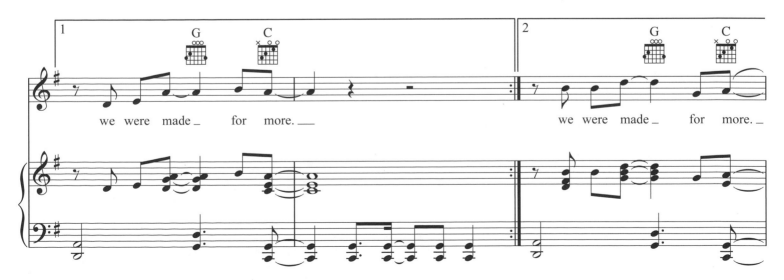

We all ___ bleed the same. ___

We're more ___ beau - ti - ful when we come to - geth - er. We all ___

bleed the same. ___ So tell me why, tell me why we're di -

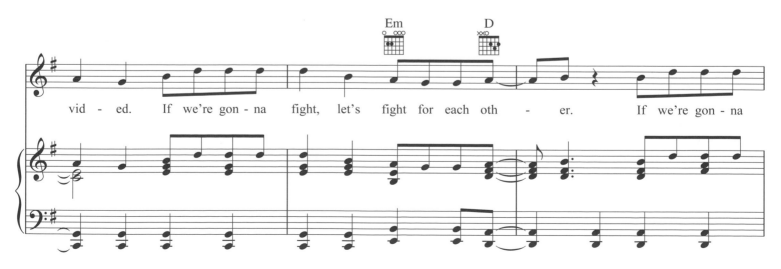

vid - ed. If we're gon - na fight, let's fight for each oth - er. If we're gon - na

shout, let love be the cry. _____ We all ___ bleed the same. _____

Let's stand u - nit - ed, let's stand u - nit - ed.

(Spoken:) So, Father God, I pray that our families will come together right now and seek Your face.

You will forgive our sins and You'll heal our incredible land. In the name of the only Savior, Jesus, Christ, Amen.

THE GOSPEL

Words and Music by BRYAN FOWLER,
TOBY McKEEHAN and RYAN STEVENSON

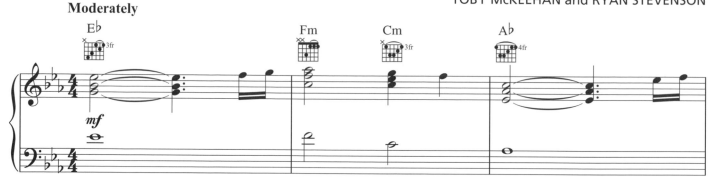

A rest-less gen-er-a-tion, we're turn-ing o-ver ev-'ry stone, __

hop-ing to find __ sal-va-tion in a world that's left us cold. __ Can we

get back to the al-tar, back to the arms of our __ first love? __ There's on-ly

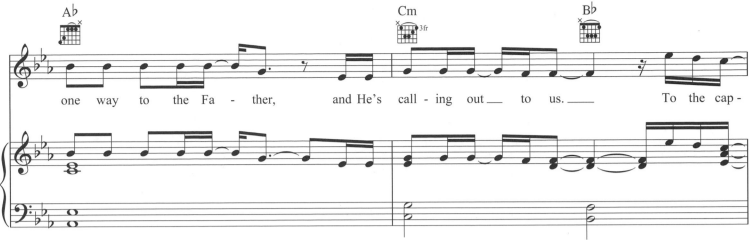

one way to the Fa - ther, and He's call - ing out ___ to us. ___ To the cap-

- tive it looks like free - dom, to the or - phan it feels like home. To the skep-

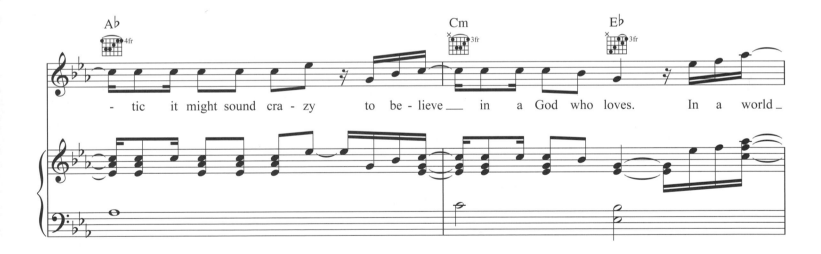

- tic it might sound cra - zy to be - lieve ___ in a God who loves. In a world ___

___ where our hearts are break - ing, and we're lost ___ in the mess we've made, like a blind-

-ing light_ in the dead_ of night,_ it's the Gos - pel, the Gos - pel that makes a way._

It's the Gos - pel that makes a way._

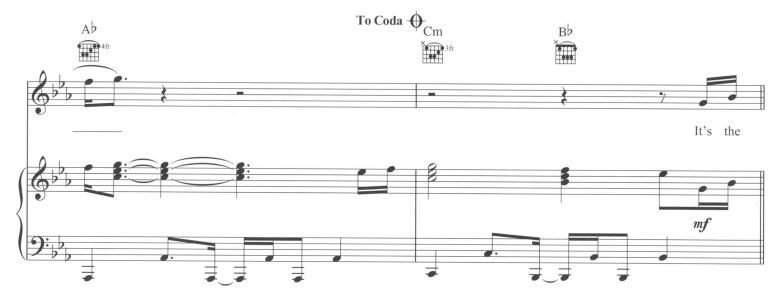

It's the

cure for our con - di - tion, it's the Good News for us all. __ It's

great-er than re-lig - ion, it's the pow-er of ___ the cross. ___ So, can we

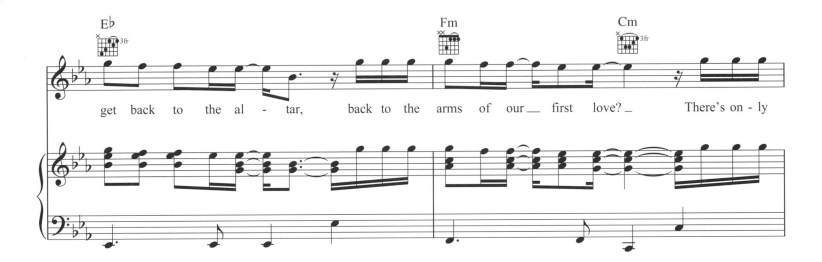

get back to the al - tar, back to the arms of our ___ first love? ___ There's on - ly

one way to the Fa - ther, and He's call - ing out ___ to us. ___ To the cap-

D.S. al Coda

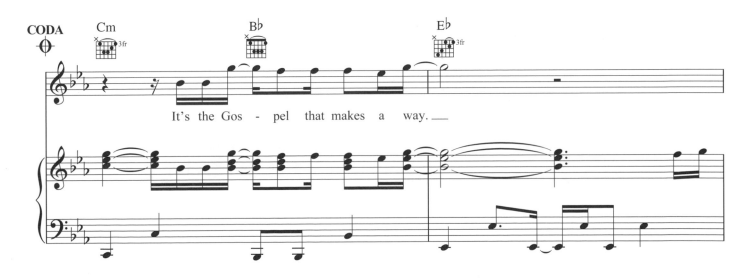

CODA

It's the Gos - pel that makes a way. ___

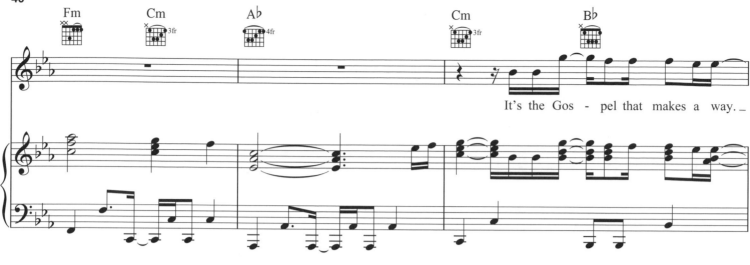

It's the Gos - pel that makes a way. _

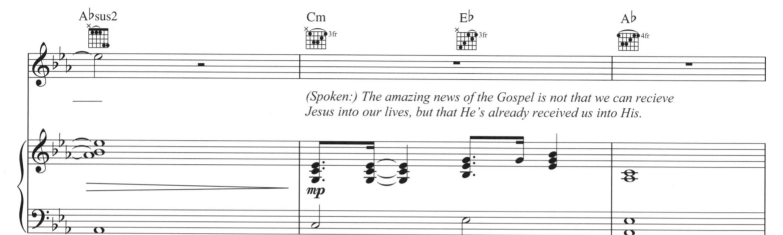

_

(Spoken:) The amazing news of the Gospel is not that we can recieve
Jesus into our lives, but that He's already received us into His.

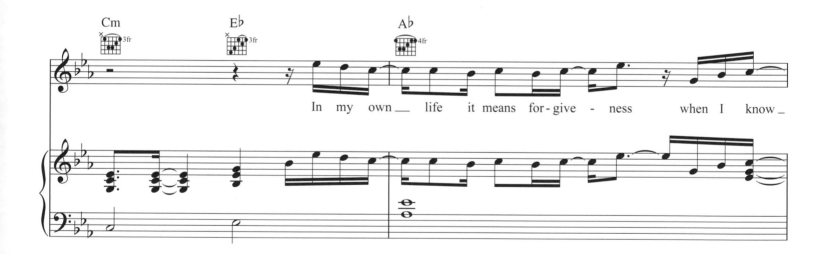

In my own _ life it means for - give - ness when I know _

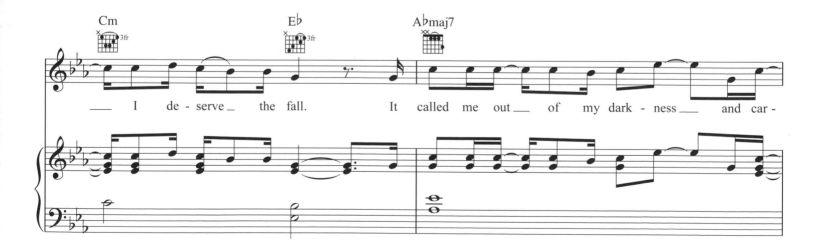

_ I de - serve _ the fall. It called me out _ of my dark - ness _ and car -

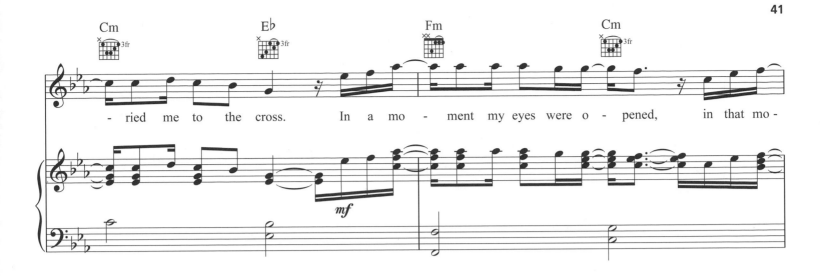

-ried me to the cross. In a mo - ment my eyes were o - pened, in that mo-

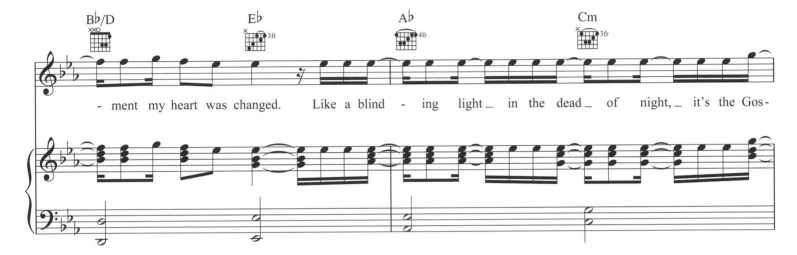

- ment my heart was changed. Like a blind - ing light _ in the dead _ of night, _ it's the Gos-

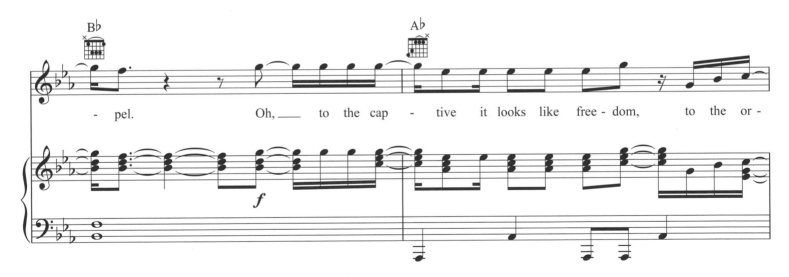

- pel. Oh, ___ to the cap - tive it looks like free - dom, to the or-

- phan it feels like home. Yeah, _ to the skep - tic it might sound cra - zy to be - lieve _

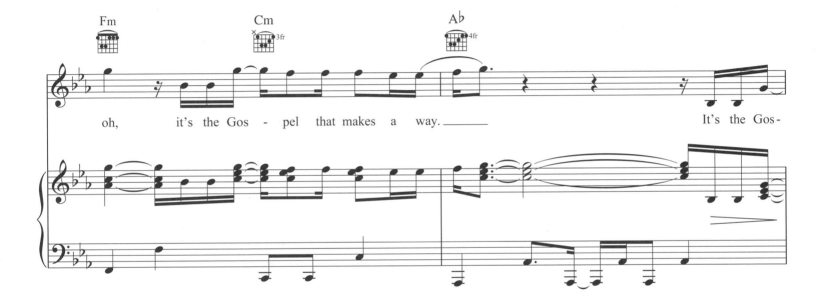

GRACEFULLY BROKEN

Words and Music by MATT REDMAN,
KATIE TORWALT, JONAS MYRIN, BRYAN TORWALT
and TASHA COBBS LEONARD

Oh, take ___ Here I am, ___ God, ___ arms ___

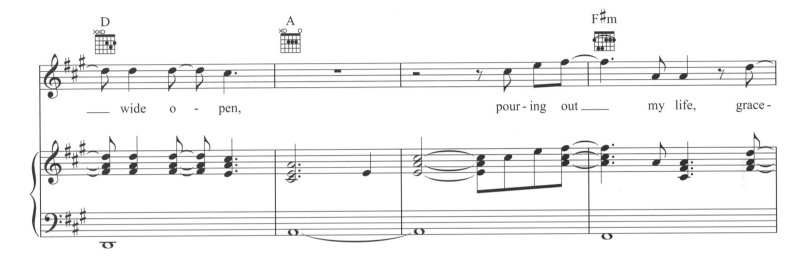

___ wide o - pen, pour - ing out ___ my life, grace -

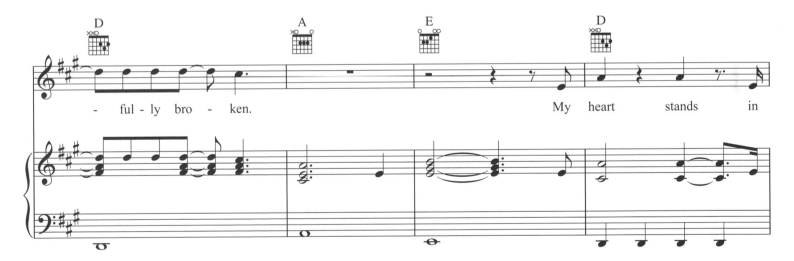

- ful - ly bro - ken. My heart stands in

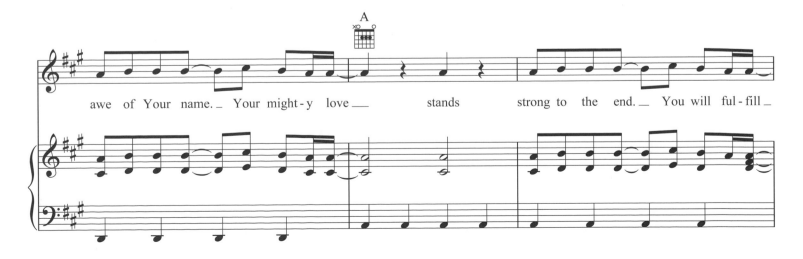

awe of Your name. ___ Your might - y love ___ stands strong to the end. ___ You will ful - fill ___

Your pur-pose for me. You won't for-sake me, You will be with

me. Here I am, God, arms wide o - pen,

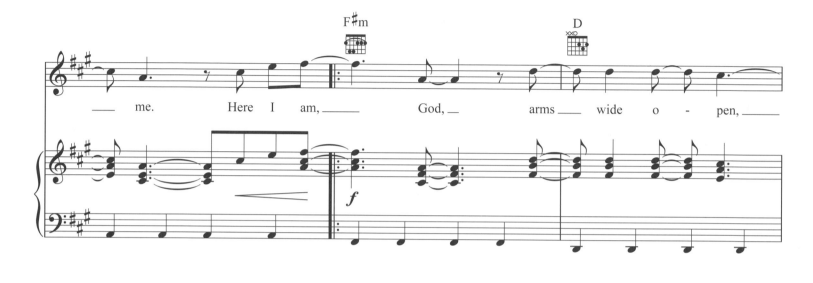

pour - ing out my life, grace-

- ful-ly bro - ken, pour-ing out my life a-gain. Here I am,

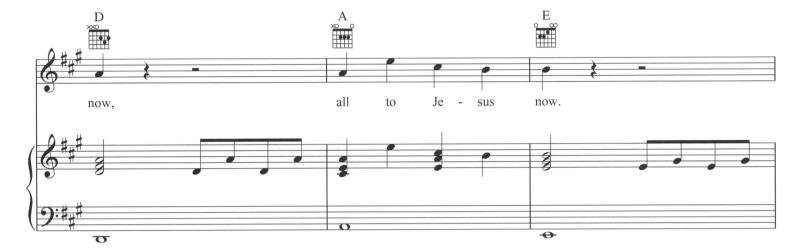

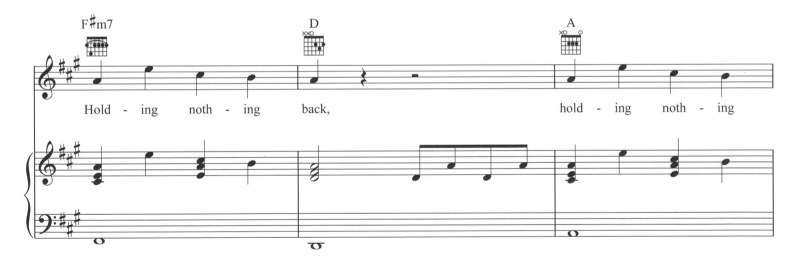

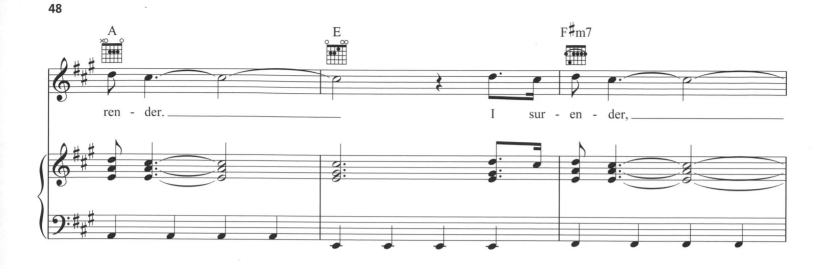

ren - der. _____ I sur - en - der, _____

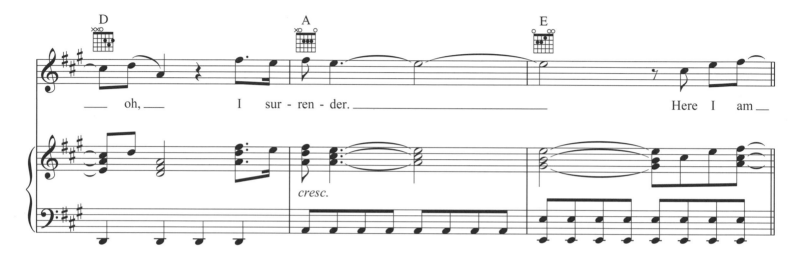

___ oh, ___ I sur - ren - der. _____ Here I am ___

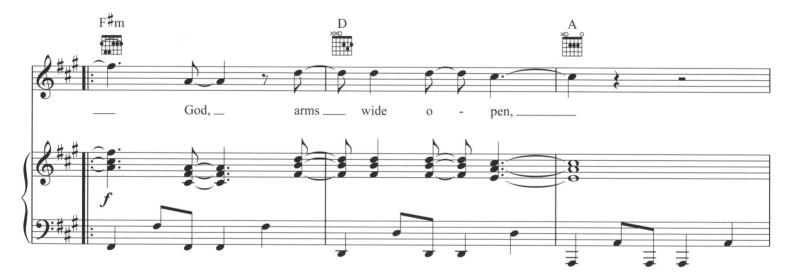

___ God, ___ arms _____ wide o - pen, _____

pour - ing out _____ my life, grace - ful - ly bro - ken, _____

GRACE GOT YOU

Words and Music by BEN GLOVER,
DAVID GARCIA, BART MILLARD,
JOHN REUBEN and SOLOMON OLDS

Moderate groove

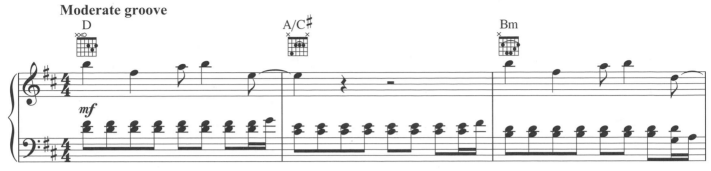

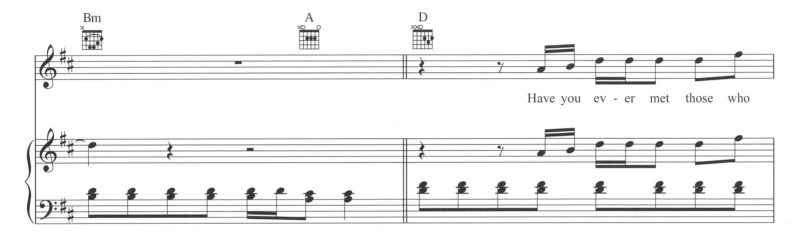

Have you ev - er met those who

keep hum-ming when the song's through? _ It's like _____

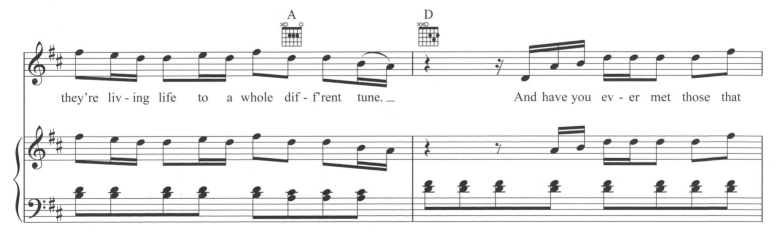

they're liv-ing life to a whole dif-f'rent tune. _ And have you ev - er met those that

keep hop-ing when it's hope-less?____ It's like____

they've fig-ured out what the rest have-n't, yeah.____ The sec-ond you re-al-ize__

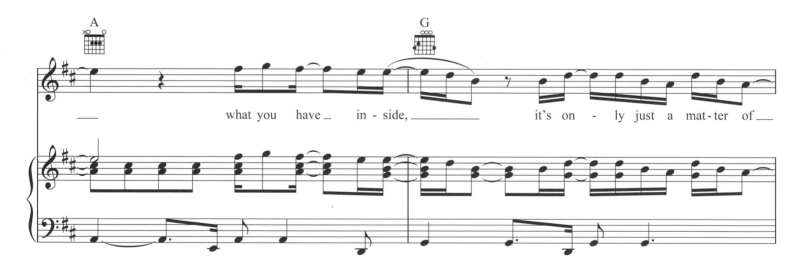

____ what you have__ in-side,_____ it's on-ly just a mat-ter of__

____ time_____ till you sing so the back row hears you. Glide, 'cause walk-ing just won't do.

Why? _____ 'Cause there ain't no storm that can change how this ends. _

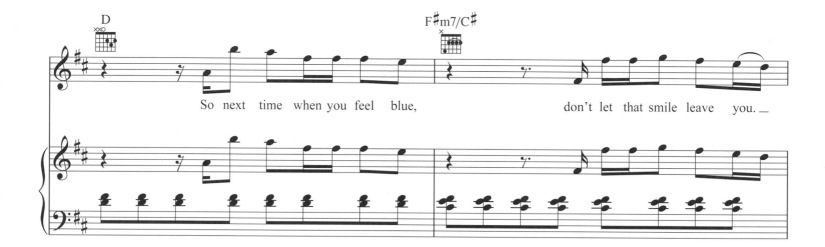

So next time when you feel blue, don't let that smile leave you. _

Why? _____ 'Cause you have ev-'ry rea-son just to

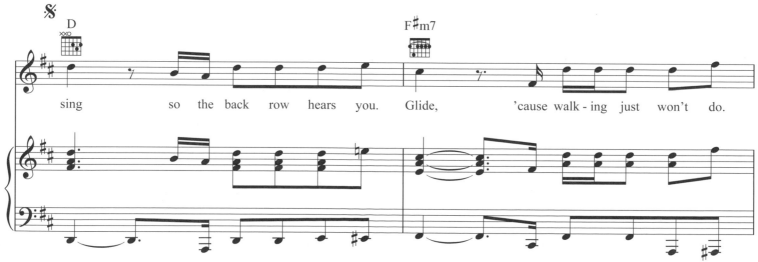

sing so the back row hears you. Glide, 'cause walk-ing just won't do.

Grace got you. *Rap: (See additional lyrics)*

Rap ends

The sec-ond you re - al - ize_____ what you have _ in - side, _

_____ it's on - ly just a mat-ter of,_____ it's on - ly just a mat-ter of___

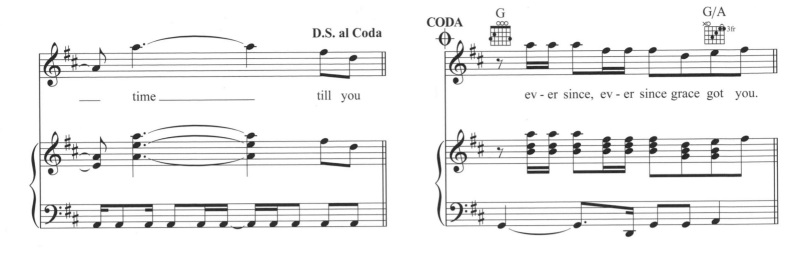

Additional Lyrics

Rap: Got away with something, bubbling inside of you,
Spilling over 'cause your life is full. How incredible!
Undeniable, monumental like the Eiffel.
Uncontrollable, let the joy flow through, ha-ha!
Giddy, oh, but pretty pretty please,
Let me see your hands in the air with you out your seats.
Warm it up, let go, shout it out, celebrate!
When you can't articulate, just say "Amazing Grace."

HOME

Words and Music by CHRIS TOMLIN,
ED CASH and SCOTT CASH

Moderate Rock feel

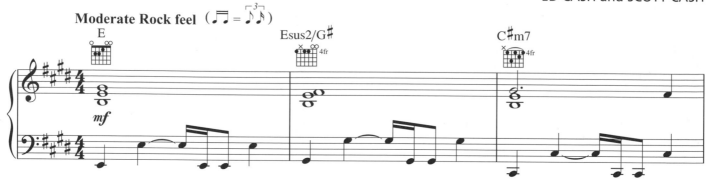

This world is not what it was meant to ___ be;

all this pain, all this suf-fer-ing. There's a bet-ter place

wait-ing ___ for ___ me in heav-en. ___

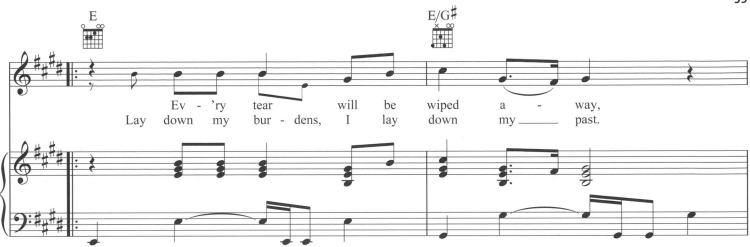

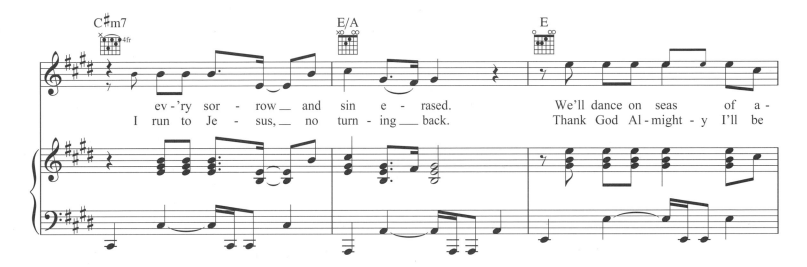

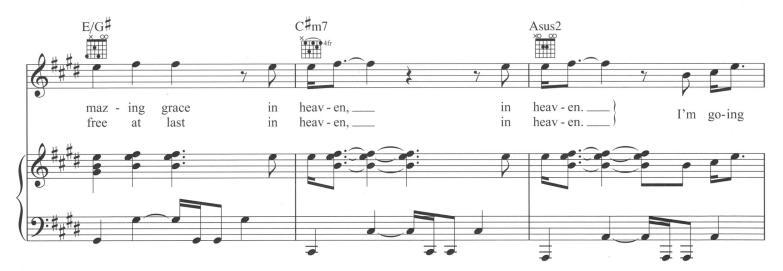

Oh, I wan - na go, __ oh, I wan - na go __ home, where ev -'ry fear is gone,

I'm in Your o - pen arms ____ where I ____ be - long. __

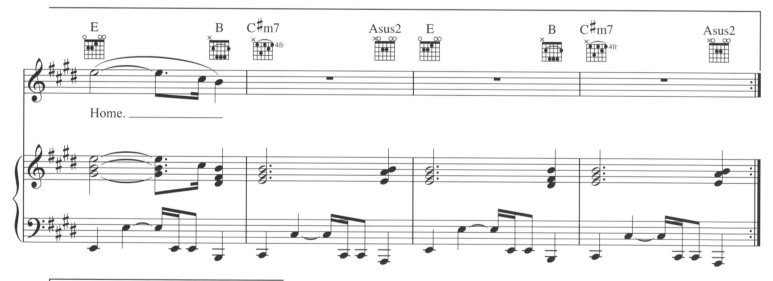

Home. ____

__ Blind - ed eyes will fi - n'lly see, the

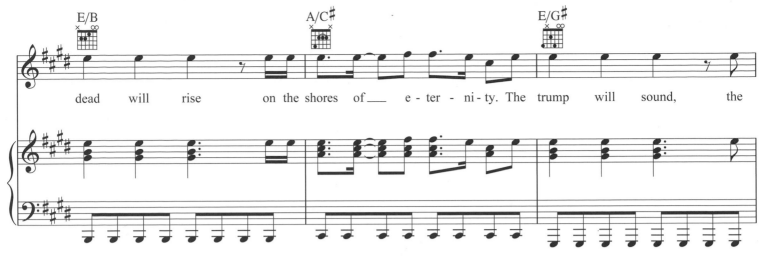

OLD CHURCH CHOIR

Words and Music by ZACH WILLIAMS,
COLBY WEDGEWORTH and ETHAN HULSE

Gospel Pop

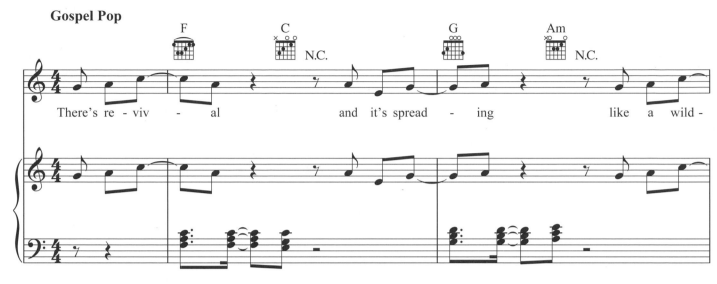

There's re-viv-al and it's spread-ing like a wild-

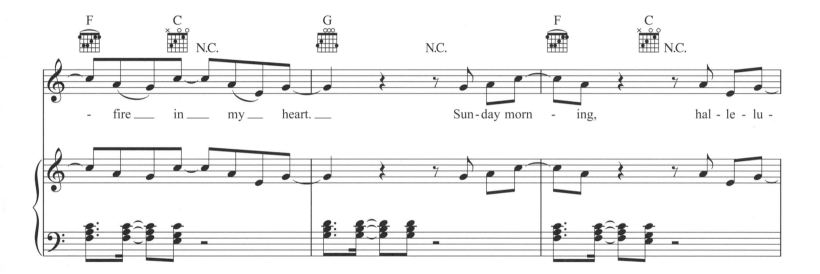

-fire __ in __ my __ heart. __ Sun-day morn - ing, hal-le-lu-

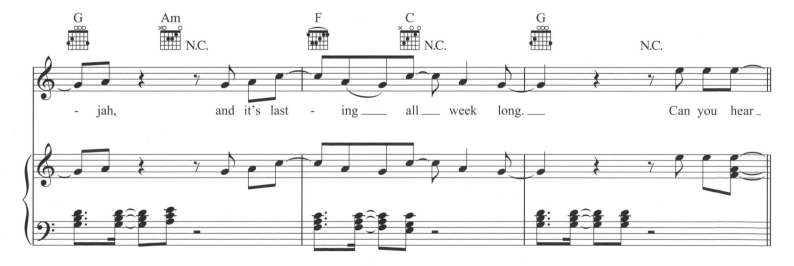

-jah, and it's last - ing __ all __ week long. __ Can you hear __

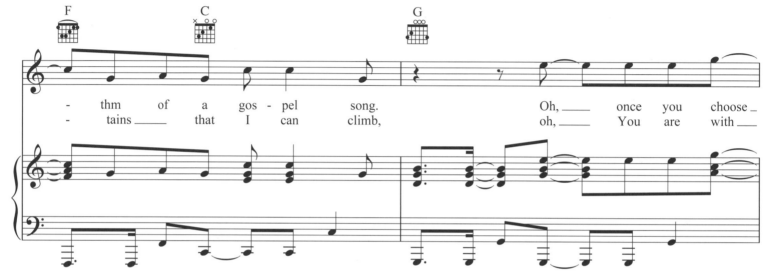

oh, _____ oh, _____ oh, _____ Clap your hands _

_ and stomp your feet till you find ___ that gos-pel beat, 'cause it's all ___ you'll ev-er need, all _

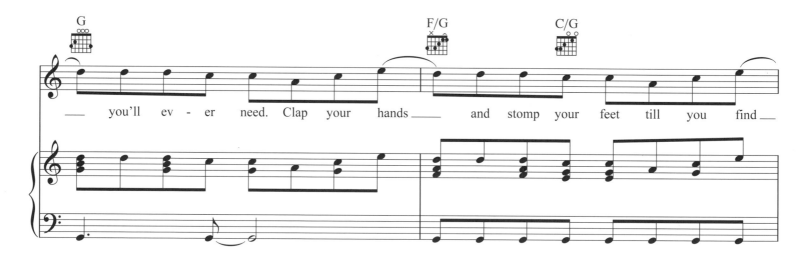

_ you'll ev-er need. Clap your hands ___ and stomp your feet till you find ___

_ that gos-pel beat, 'cause it's all ___ you'll ev-er need, all ___

MASTERPIECE

Words and Music by BERNIE HERMS
and EMILY WEISBAND

Power Ballad

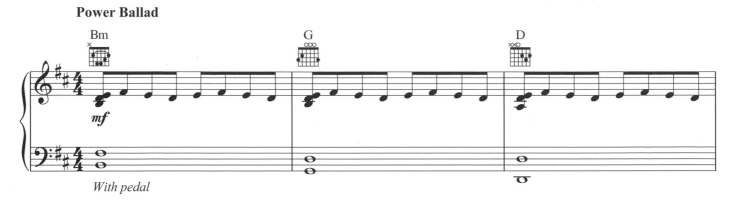

Heart - break's _ a bit - ter ___ sound.

Know it well; _ it's ring - ing in ___ my ears, and I can't un - der - stand why I'm ___ not

fixed by ____ now. Begged, and I ____ have plead-ed, "Take this pain," but I'm still bleed-ing. ____

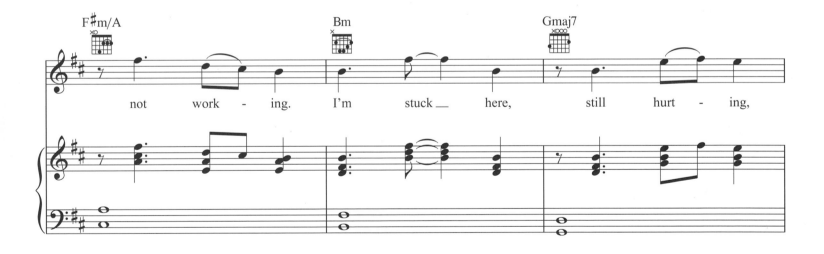

Heart trusts ____ You for cer - tain, head says ____ it's

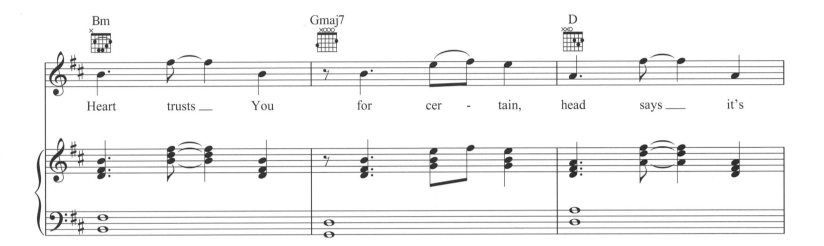

not work - ing. I'm stuck ____ here, still hurt - ing,

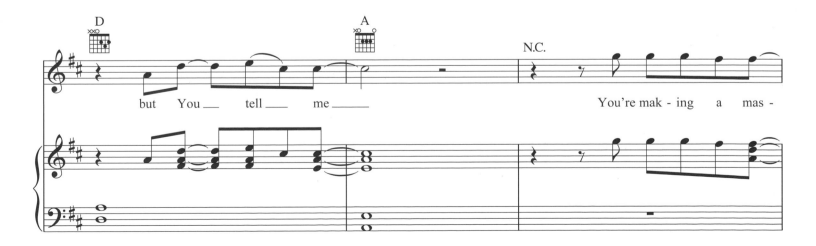

but You ___ tell ___ me ____ You're mak - ing a mas -

-ter - piece. You're shap-ing the soul ___ in me. ___ You're mov-ing where I ___

___ can't see, ___ and all ___ I am ___ is in ___ Your hands. ___

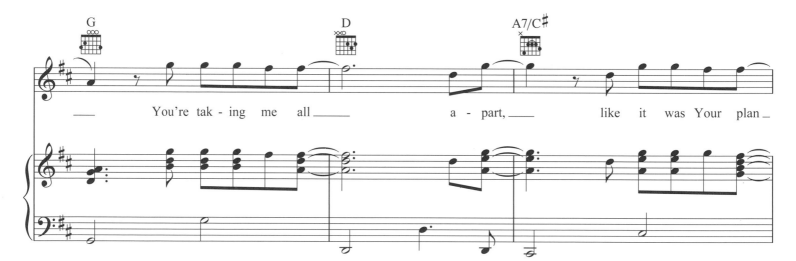

___ You're tak-ing me all ___ a - part, ___ like it was Your plan ___

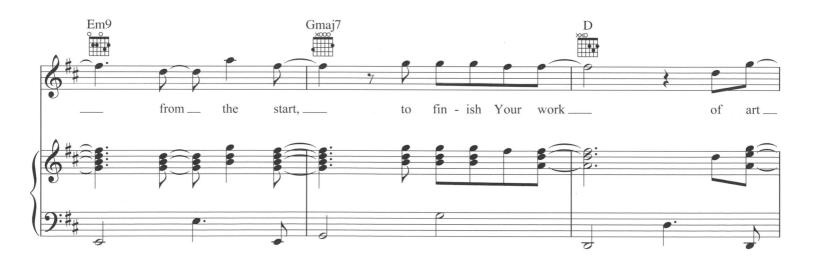

___ from ___ the start, ___ to fin - ish Your work ___ of art ___

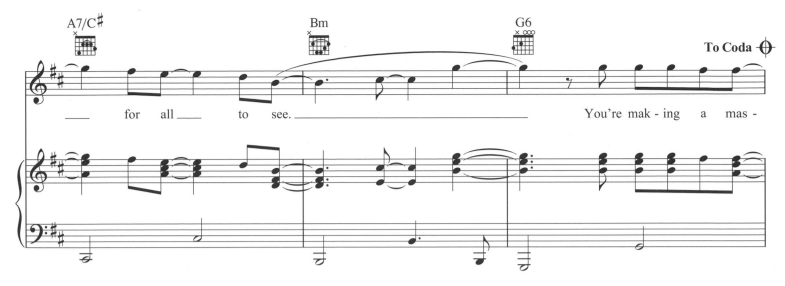

for all ___ to see. _____ You're mak-ing a mas-

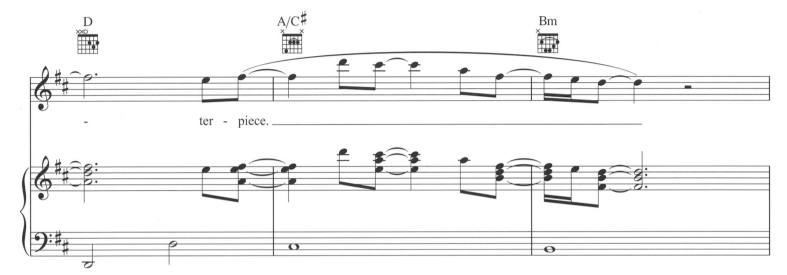

-ter - piece. _____

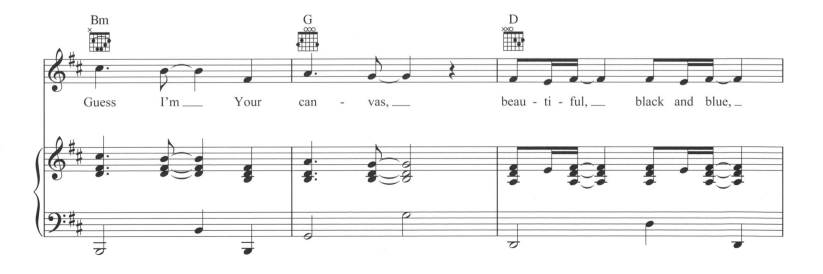

Guess I'm ___ Your can - vas, ___ beau-ti-ful, ___ black and blue, ___

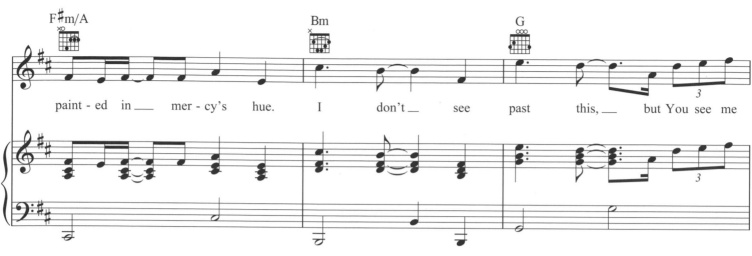

paint - ed in ___ mer - cy's hue. I don't ___ see past this, ___ but You see me

now, who I'll be then, there at the end, stand - ing there as ___ Your mas -

D.S. al Coda

CODA

- ter - piece. ___

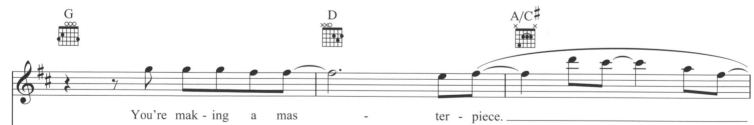

You're mak - ing a mas - ter - piece. ___

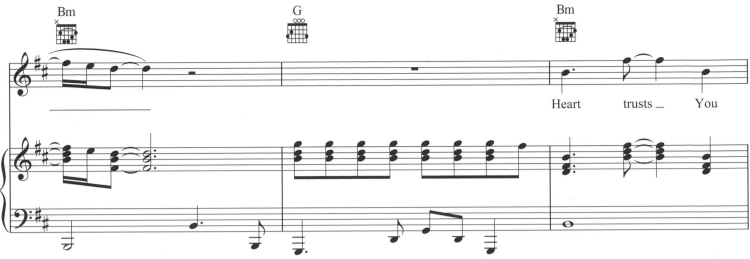

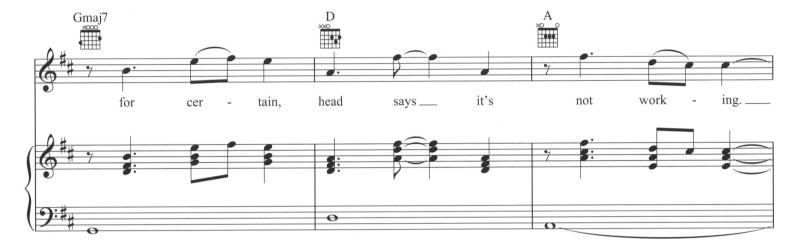

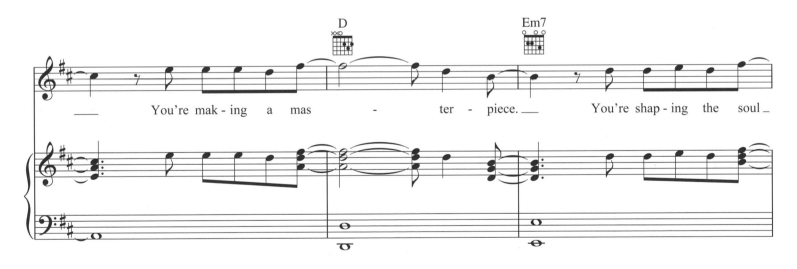

see, ___ and all ___ I am ___ is in ___ Your hands. ___

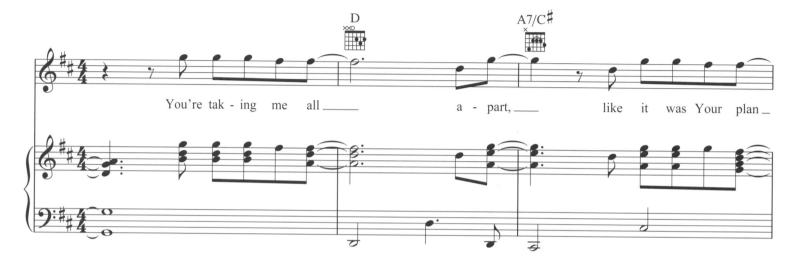

You're tak - ing me all ___ a - part, ___ like it was Your plan __

___ from ___ the start, ___ to fin - ish Your work ___ of art __

___ for all ___ to see. ___ You're mak - ing a mas -

MORE THAN ANYTHING

Words and Music by SAMUEL MIZELL
and BECCA MIZELL

Recorded a half step lower.

take my pain a - way. ___ But, e - ven if you don't, I ___ pray: ___ help me want the

Heal - er ___ more than the heal - ing. ___ Help me want the

Sav - ior ___ more than the sav - ing. ___ Help me want the

Giv - er ___ more than the giv - ing. Oh, help me want You,

To Coda ⊕

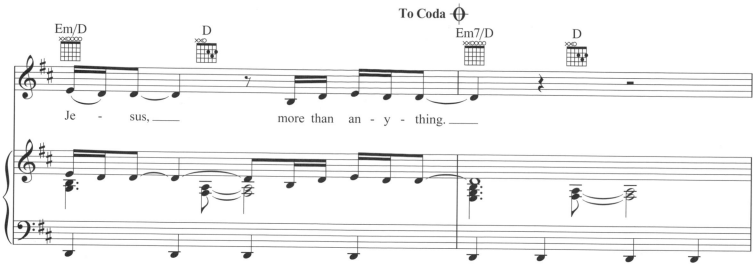

Je - sus, _____ more than an - y - thing. _____

You know more than an - y - one that my flesh is weak, _____

and You know I'd give _____ an - y - thing _____ for a rem - e - dy. _____

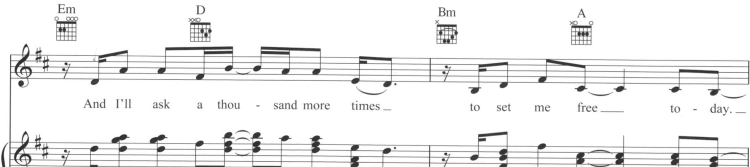

And I'll ask a thou - sand more times _____ to set me free _____ to - day. _____

Oh, ___ but, e-ven if you don't, I ___ pray: ___ help me want the

When I'm des-p'rate and

my heart's o-ver-come, ___ all that I need ___ You've

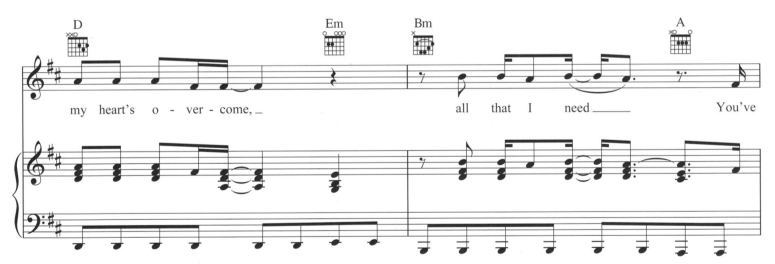

al-read-y done, ___ oh. ___ When I'm des-p'rate ___ and

heal - ing. _____ Help me want the Sav - ior _____ more than the

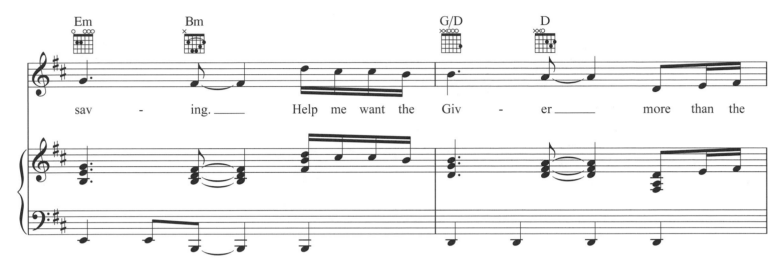

sav - ing. _____ Help me want the Giv - er _____ more than the

giv - ing. ___ Oh, help me want You, Je - sus, ___ more than an - y - thing. _

Help _ me want You, Je - sus, _ more than an - y - thing. ___

rit.

NEVER BEEN
(Never Been a Moment)

Words and Music by JEFF PARDO
and MICAH TYLER

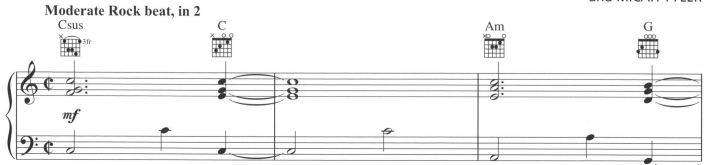

I've _____ been a sin-ner, I've _____ been a saint, a lit-l
_____ been the rock, _____ You've _____ been the peace, al-

-tle bit of both ev-'ry sin-gle day. I've been lost, _____ but some-
-ways show-ing Your good heart to me. My days are marked _____ by grace _____

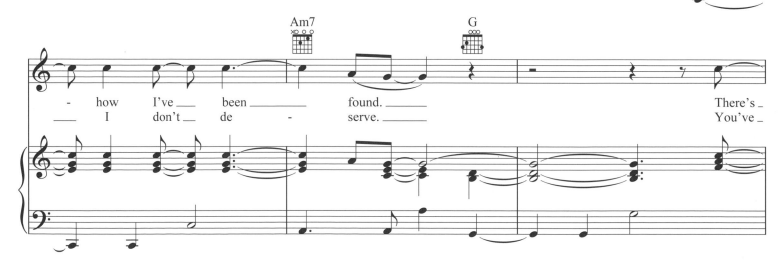

-how I've _____ been _____ found. _____ There's
_____ I don't _____ de - serve. _____ You've _____

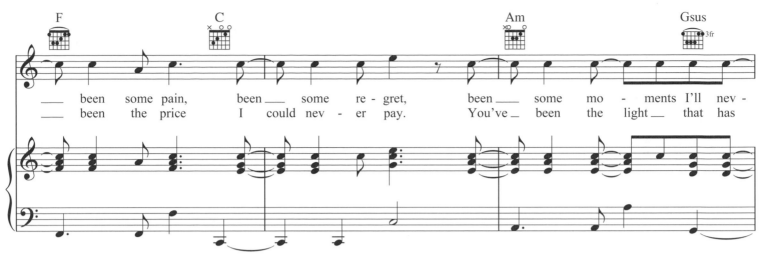

been some pain, been some re-gret, been some mo-ments I'll nev-
been the price I could nev-er pay. You've been the light that has

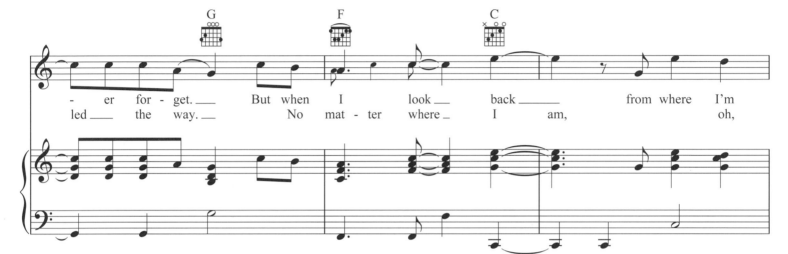

-er for-get. But when I look back from where I'm
led the way. No mat-ter where I am, oh,

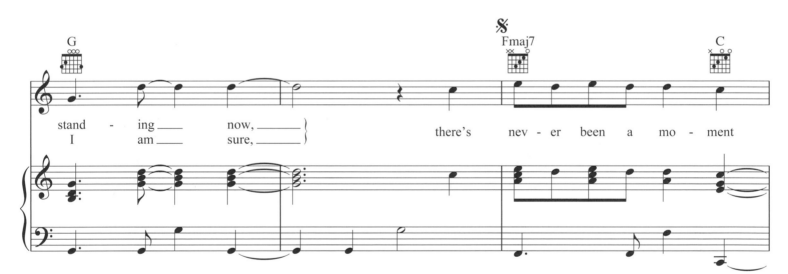

stand-ing now, there's nev-er been a mo-ment
I am sure,

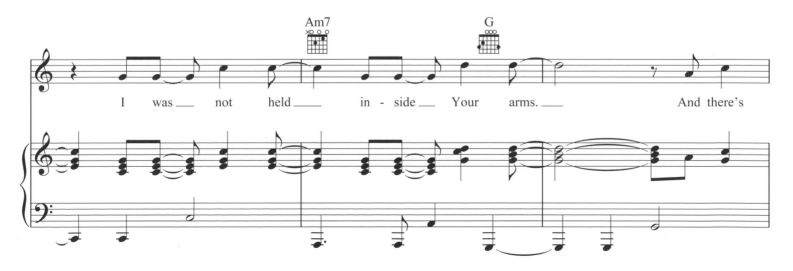

I was not held in-side Your arms. And there's

nev-er been a day when You were — not who — You say — You are.

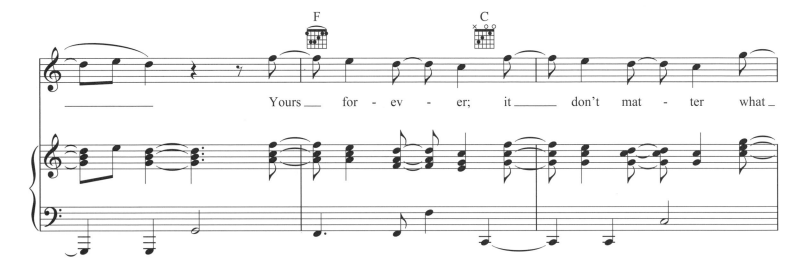

_____ Yours — for-ev-er; it _____ don't mat-ter what _

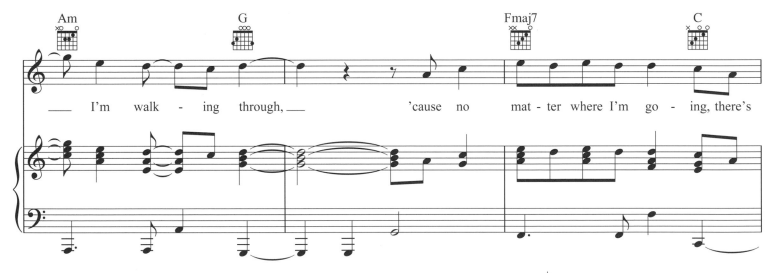

___ I'm walk-ing through, ___ 'cause no mat-ter where I'm go-ing, there's

nev-er been a mo-ment that I was not loved by ___ You.

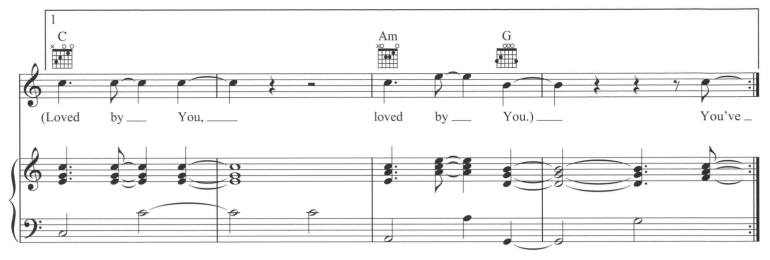

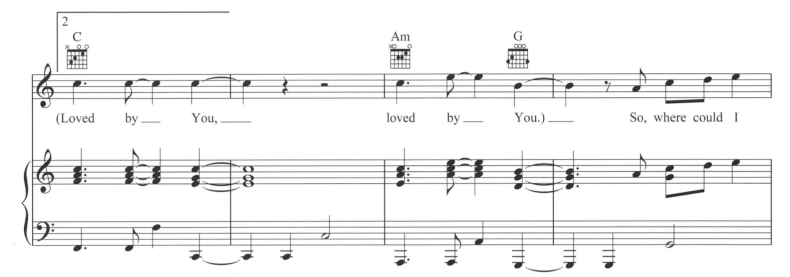

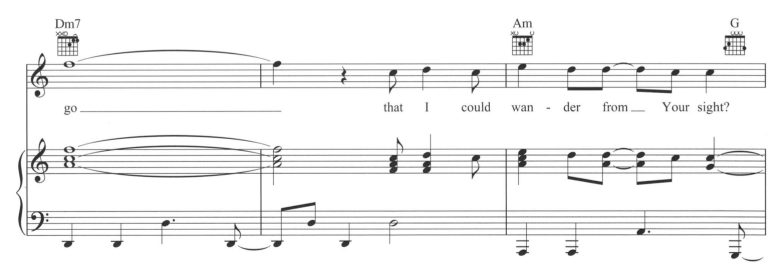

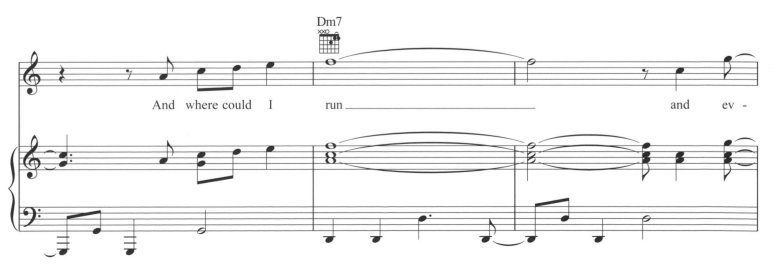

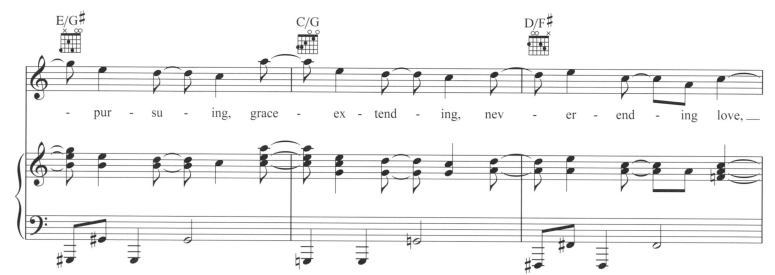

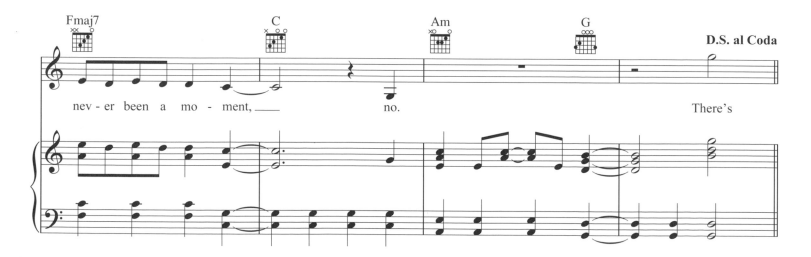

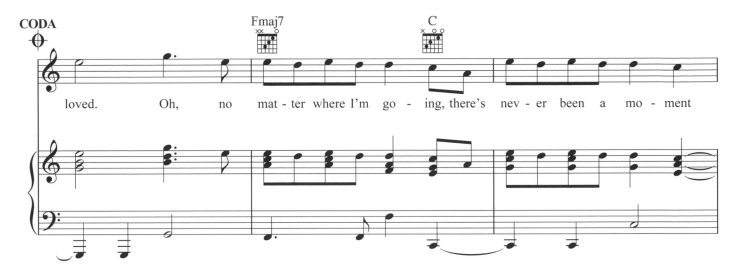

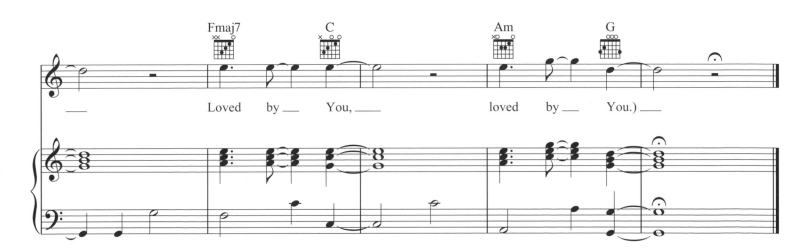

NO ONE LIKE OUR GOD

Words and Music by LINCOLN BREWSTER,
CORBIN PHILLIPS and TAYLOR GALL

Moderate Rock beat

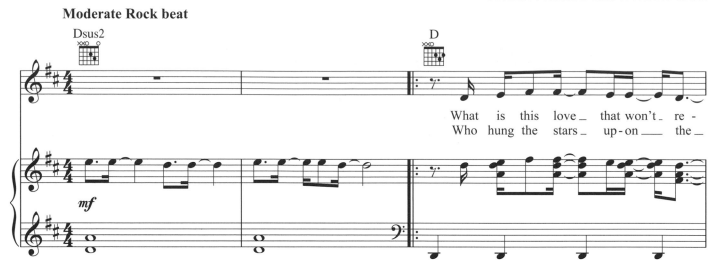

What is this love _ that won't re-
Who hung the stars _ up-on ___ the _

- lent,
___ night,

that's call-ing out _ with heav - en's ___ breath?
and showed the sun _ how bright _ to ___ shine?

Who's reach-ing wide _ to save _ our ___ souls?   On - ly   You, _
Who shaped the world _ with-in ___ His ___ hands?   On - ly   You, _

ooh.
ooh.

What is this grace ___ that makes ___ no ___
Who set the sky ___ a - bove ___ the ___

___ sense,
___ hills,

that we could nev - er re - com - pense?
and told the wa - ters to ___ be ___ still?

Who gives us all ___ a sec - ond ___ chance? On - ly You, ___
Who spoke to form ___ the u - ni - verse? On - ly You, ___

___ on - ly You, ___ on - ly You. ___
___ on - ly You, ___ on - ly You. ___

There is no one like our God.

save. There is no one like our God.
No

height or depth can stand be - tween ___ us. No pow'r on earth or

all cre - a - tion, nor life or death can sep - a - rate ___ us from

Your love. ___
No height or depth can

stand be - tween __ us. No pow'r on earth or all cre - a - tion, nor

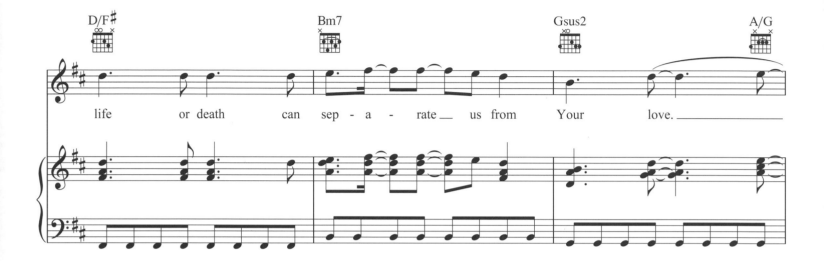

life or death can sep - a - rate __ us from Your love. _____

__ There is no one like our God. There is

no one like our __ God. There is no oth - er God who __ can

save. There is no one like our God. There is

no one like our God. There is no oth - er God who __ can

save. There is save. There is no one like our God.

OH MY SOUL

Words and Music by JOHN MARK HALL,
BERNIE HERMS and NICHOLE NOREDEMAN

Moderately, in 2

Oh,   my
Here   and

soul,   oh, how you wor - ry.   Oh, how you're wea - ry from fear - ing you
now,   you can be hon - est.   I won't try to prom - ise that some - day it

Oh, my soul, you are not a-

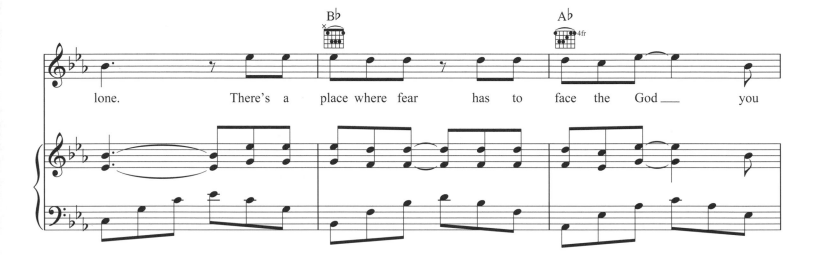

lone. There's a place where fear has to face the God __ you

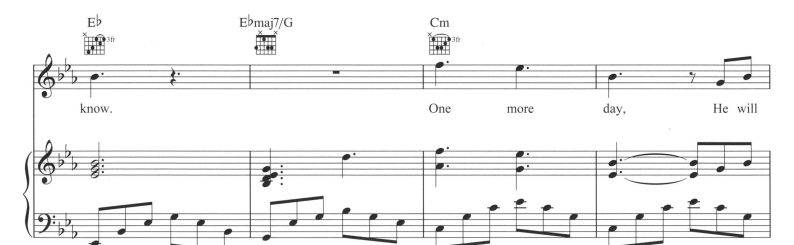

know. One more day, He will

make __ a way. Let Him show you how you can

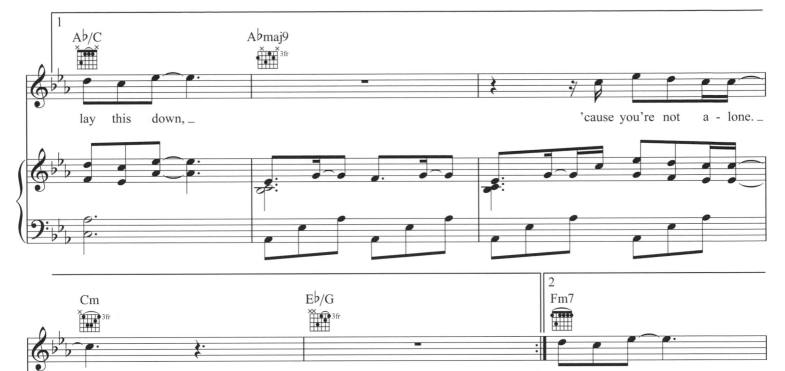

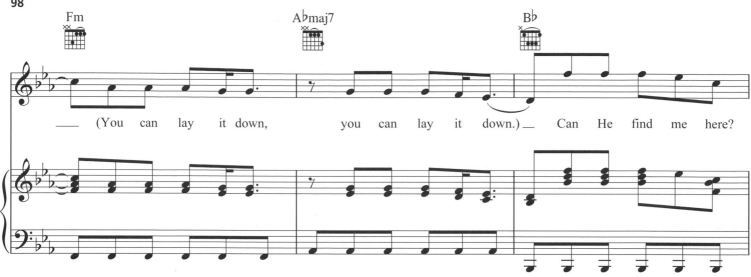

(You can lay it down, you can lay it down.) __ Can He find me here?

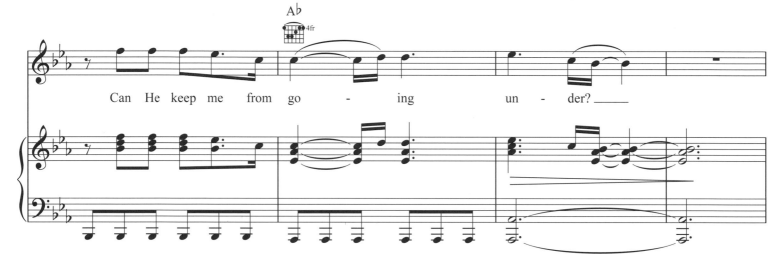

Can He keep me from go - ing un - der? _____

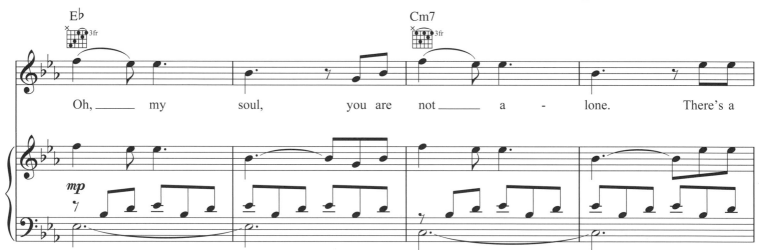

Oh, _____ my soul, you are not _____ a - lone. There's a

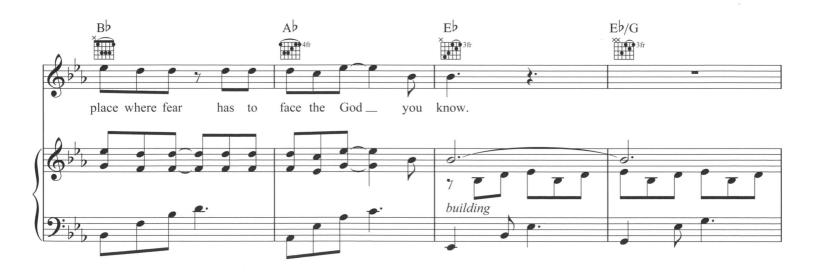

place where fear has to face the God __ you know.

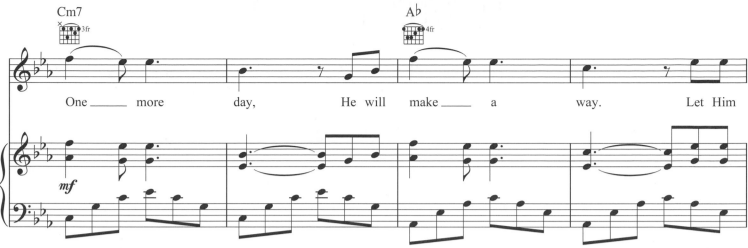

One ___ more day, He will make ___ a way. Let Him

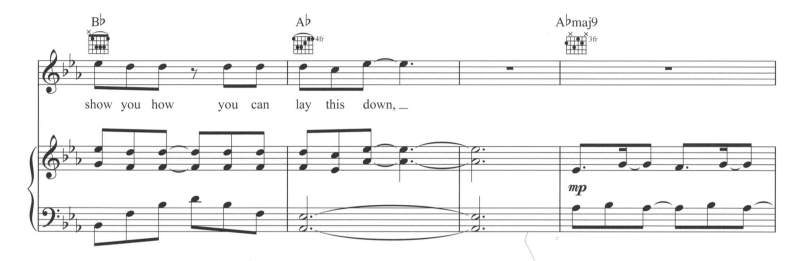

show you how you can lay this down, __

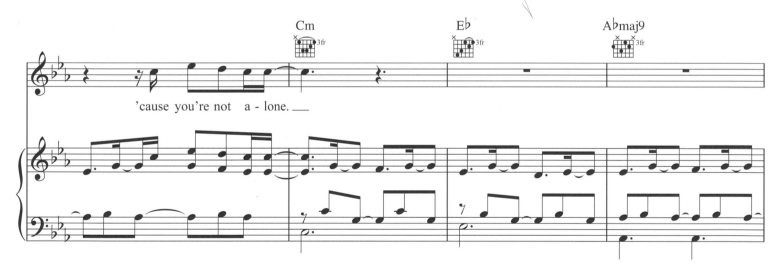

'cause you're not a - lone. __

Oh, my soul, you're not a - lone.

WORD OF LIFE

Words and Music by JEREMY CAMP,
ETHAN HULSE and COLBY WEDGEWORTH

Moderate Rock beat

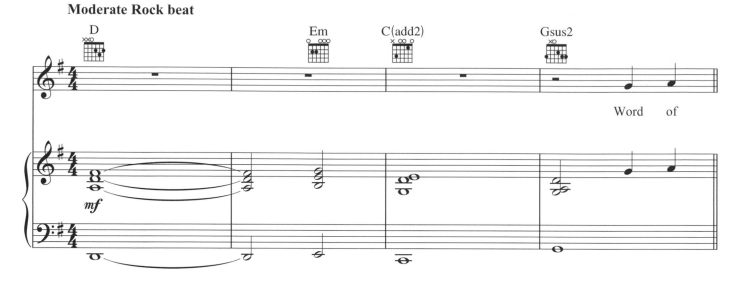

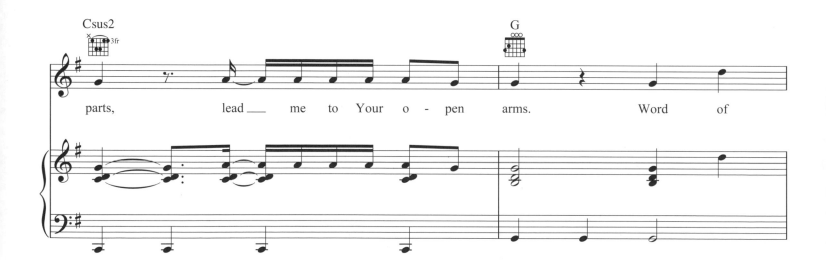

Truth, __ il - lu - mi - nate all these lies the en - e - my speaks in -

side. In free - dom, I __ will rise. __ 'Cause You called me out __

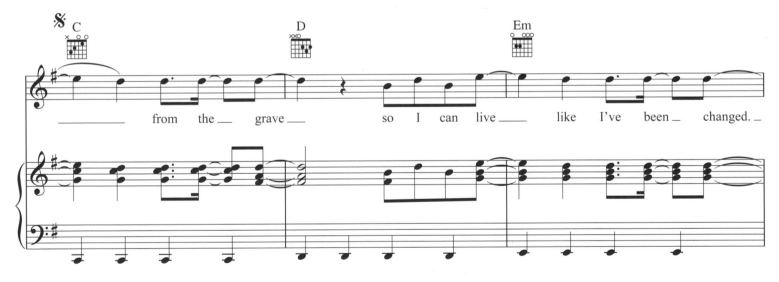

__ from the __ grave __ so I can live __ like I've been __ changed. __

__ There is a new __ song in my __ soul, __ and it be - gins __

God, ___ fill ___ me with joy a - gain, ___ spring - ing up from with -

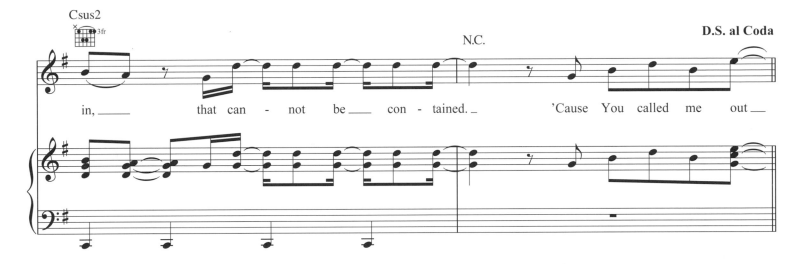

in, ___ that can - not be ___ con - tained. ___ 'Cause You called me out ___

D.S. al Coda

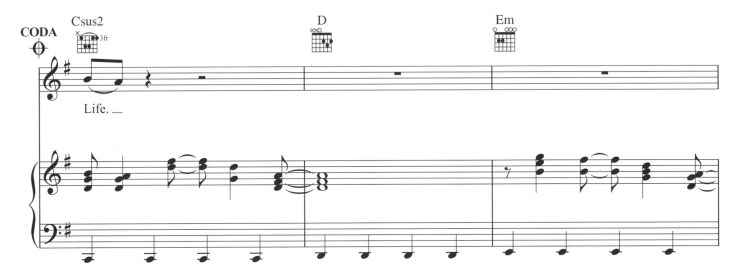

CODA

Life. ___

The old has gone a - way; on - ly Your love re - mains.

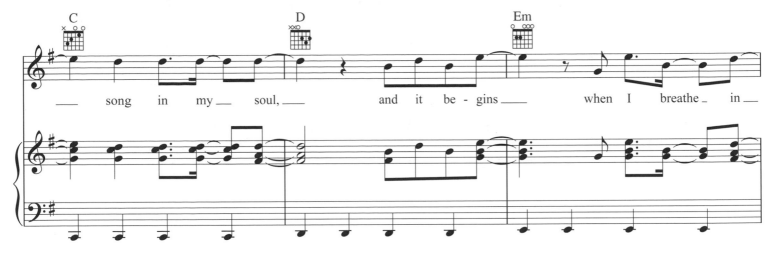

song in my soul, and it be-gins when I breathe in

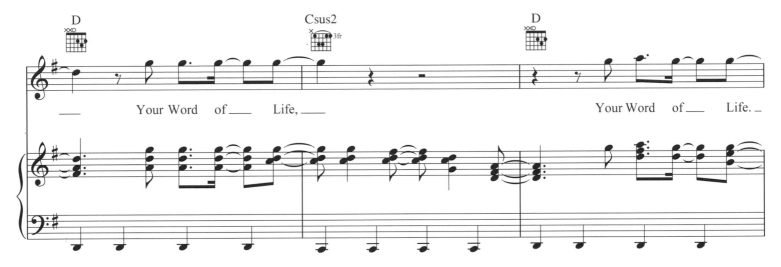

Your Word of Life, Your Word of Life.

Hey, the old has gone a-way;

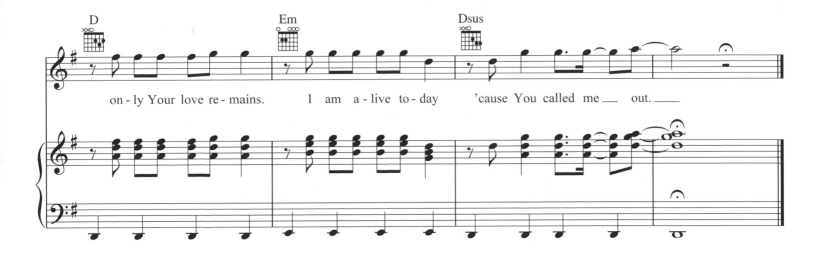

on - ly Your love re - mains. I am a - live to - day 'cause You called me out.

RESURRECTION POWER

Words and Music by ED CASH,
RYAN ELLIS and TONY BROWN

Moderately slow

You called me from the grave by name.

You called me out of all my shame. I see the old has

passed a-way, ___ the new has come. ___

Recorded a half step higher.

Now I have res - ur - rec - tion

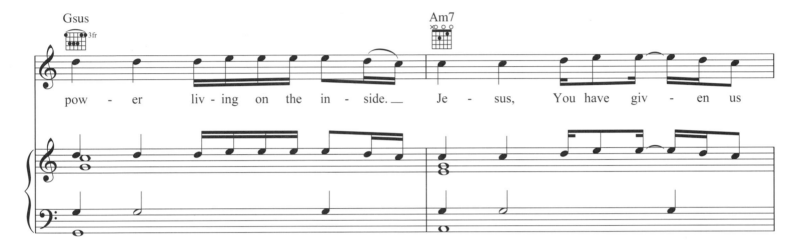

pow - er liv - ing on the in - side.___ Je - sus, You have giv - en us

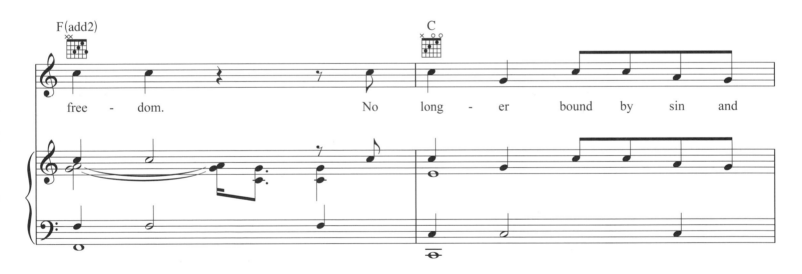

free - dom. No long - er bound by sin and

dark - ness; liv - ing in the light of Your___ good - ness, You have giv - en us

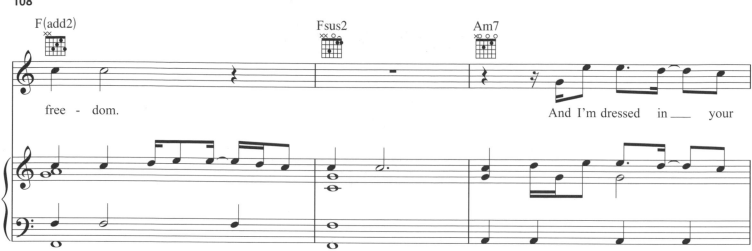

free - dom.   And I'm dressed in ___ your

roy - al - ty;   Your Ho - ly Spir - it   lives   in   me.

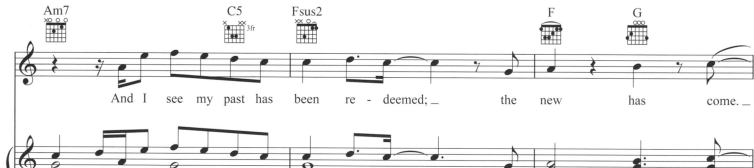

And I see my past has been re - deemed; ___ the new has come. ___

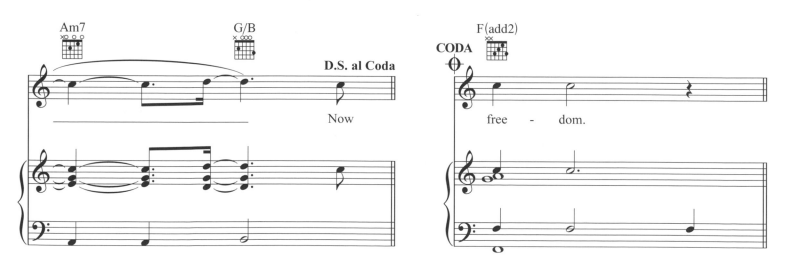

D.S. al Coda

Now

CODA

free - dom.

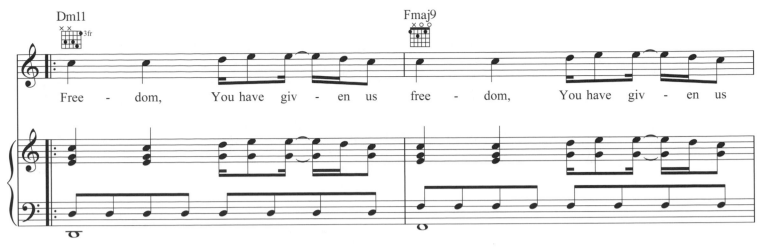

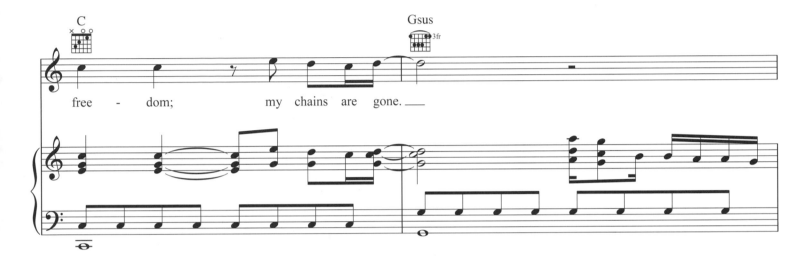

free - dom; hal - le - lu - jah. _____ Now _____

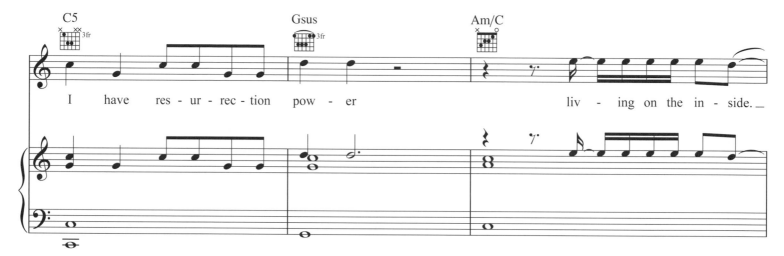

I have res - ur - rec - tion pow - er liv - ing on the in - side. _

_____ And I'm no long - er bound by sin and

dark - ness; liv - ing in the light of Your good - ness, You have giv - en us

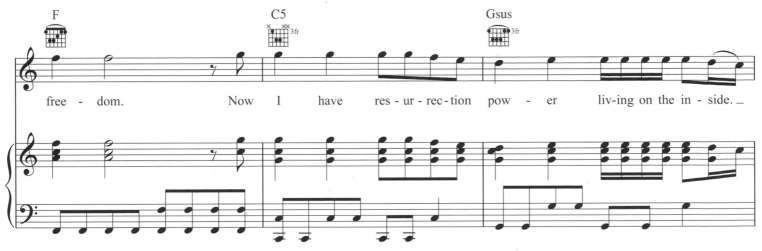

freedom. Now I have res-ur-rec-tion pow - er liv-ing on the in - side. __

Je - sus, You have giv - en us free - dom. And I'm no

long - er bound by sin and dark - ness; liv - ing in the light of Your __

good - ness, You have giv - en us free - dom. I have res - ur - rec-tion

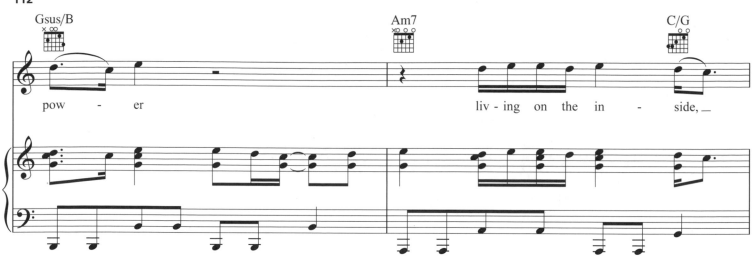

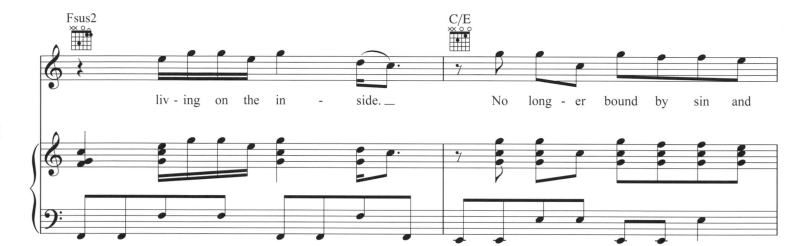

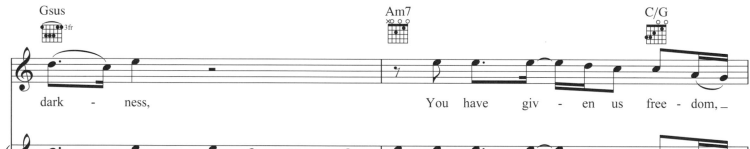